Wall Street Occupied

TheFanNJ: Omar Dyer

![Occupy Wall Street protesters on steps]

The Next Generation of Leaders Documentary Volume 3

Publisher: Coaches! 101 A NJ-Non-Profit
Acquisitions Editor: TheFanNJ
Production: Createspace
Photo Editor: Coaches! 101 Media
Senior Author: Omar Dyer
Publishing distribution: Amazon

PUBLISHED COACHES! 101, INC
PO Box 4463 Jersey City NJ 07304
www.coaches101.org
Jersey City NJ, 07305

Library of Congress Control Number:

2011962093

Note: Library of Congress Control Numbers (LCCNs) assigned beginning January 2001 have the following format: 2001012345. Please print the control number exactly as it appears above. Do not add a hyphen.

Printed in the United States of America!

Please notify us immediately of any change in the bibliographic information pertaining to your forthcoming book so that we update our database to maintain accurate information.

Written by Omar Dyer for those occupying cities in America

In these difficult times, we are burdened by the lack of transparency in government. And this continuous notion, that all men, women and children are created equal – is now subjected to the feasible face on what is called wealth. The true economic disparity in this country (America) is the accumulation of wealth, and what can buy a life of lavishness. In the 50's people marched and came together and protested for their political rights to make living more affordable, and wages more competitive. In a notion that if you worked hard, achieved and drove for a better life, your achievements were honored. Yet, in these last sub-par years (30) or more we have seen the economic situation and challenges of the few grow worse, and the healing process, became relevant to how much you can pay, or how little you owe.

Yes, we have a large distribution of wealth in the tax codes that favor the upper class – as we also have a lack of art distribution, as we are seeing that literary arts, recreation and other non-financial entities are struggling. Not the entertainment industry, which seems to thieve in tough economic situations. As photographic images, adultery, and other forms of naughty entertainment has become the fashion of life. Exotic entertainment is not a sin, but an extension of living wealth.

Yet, we are now looking at a moment in time where a generation is standing up, and fighting against the exclusion of a poverish nation. And as seen in past-times, when people who are poor; look to speak out against the privileged or the wealthy – many times these brave citizens, are casted as out-laws, or criminals. If you're apart of the nation's lowest point, where economic wealth is rapidly falling from your reach, when getting an education becomes harder, and harder--while earning a good salary becomes an inevitable challenge due to wealth distribution—or when a dream of a better living becomes the pathway challenge.

And you find yourself occupying a city, to protest against the unjust – live up to that potential that the dream of America is still there. And you see people with different faces, different creed – different beliefs coming together in solidarity for one global cause: you must ask yourself, are these people out laws or are they fighters. This letter or blog is to inspire the electric – on standing up for democracy, and believing in the truth: since this is what democracy looks like.

Democracy is when people start movements, as to when they have had enough of the greed – corruption, and they have had enough of the black plague. Which is poverty, as it is said in the scripts a plague will strike the earth. Yet, it didn't say the sickness was a virus: and this can be our plague: which is wealth distribution. Since man made the rules on material item, such as money – while making things harder for those who have not: plus making it easier for those that have.

Table of Content:

Chapter 1:

Letters from Protesting on
Wall Street

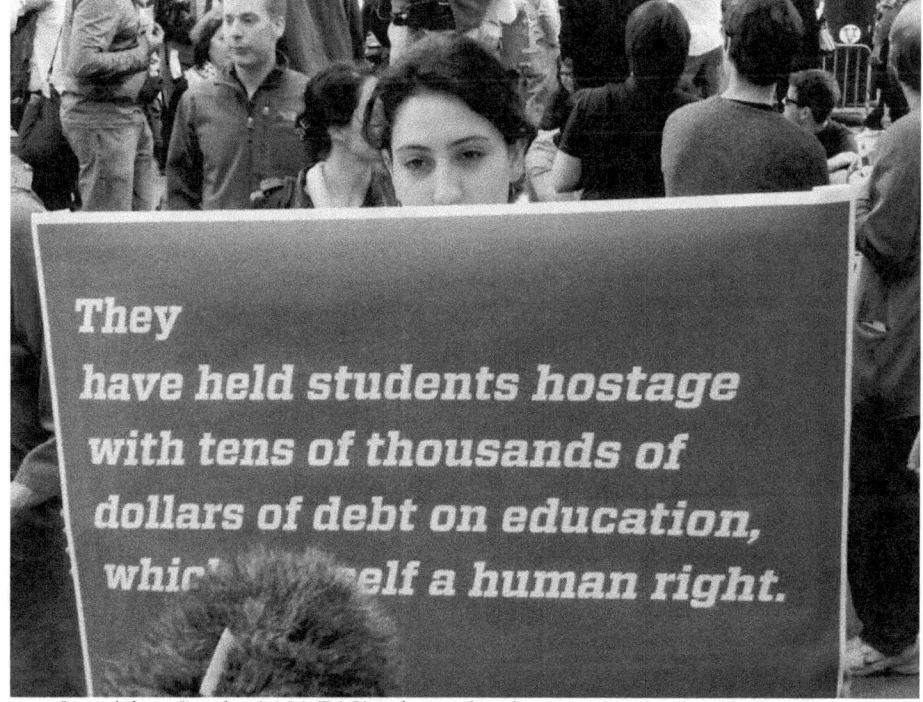

Copyrights: Coaches! 101 (PAC) : photo taken by Omar Dyer: a.k.a TheFanNJ:
Zuccotti Park New York City 10/2011

Occupy Wall Street: Letters from Wall Street Protesters

In September of 2011: a few brave people, students – low income families, protesters: civil rights activist, and anyone who embodies themselves as the 99%. Joined a general assembly to create an occupation of cities around the world! Where the goal was to raise enough awareness to allow the people on uniting for the oppression of the upper class? People always wanted to know who is a part of this movement, what is this movement about—plus what are they protesting for or on.

I am Omar Dyer also known as TheFanNJ when doing documentaries on significant events. Many of my webisodes or web-com, is widely known for on the point and right in the face content– they are short-films done on live public places like YouTube. When I heard about the Occupy Wall Street movement, I needed to know what they were protesting about? And I wanted to know why they are out there fighting hard for civilian rights – since the media was projecting their rights to protest in a different view or agenda, on what is really happening with a peaceful demonstration of civil rights. Nor did I know, or have I would have known – that the stories and feelings of the people in this movement are at the tables of every single person in this world.

In this narrated short film / documentary; I will talk about what this movement meant to the people who classify themselves as members of the 99%. And what my ambitions are will be to explain, how captivating and try to bring light—on some of the most important factors are for those: who are the 99%. In a move to mandate some of the leaders involved in this monumental movement of like minded people, trying to organize and monitor what we call Occupy Wall Street. And like any other movement there needs to be a starting point, an entry point, a beginning—plus an end in order to allocate the meaning of the protest.

Scene 1: Student Loans

Narrator:

Joining a movement with a group of passionate citizens became a calling method for The Next Generation of Leaders' Movement. And life went on as usual for those that lived in NYC's Manhattan Borough. Time Square New York, which is always a packed place – has now become the center of attention. What's going on that makes this place so special outside of the normal or everyday events? Besides the Broadway spectacle shows, the movies – bars with live entertainment – or the lights, in action: with cameras all over stealing the masque glare. People were looking for something in Time Square: what they were looking for in a moment become too great to lose sight on spotting a celebrity, but yet, being caught in an independent script.

I am TheFanNJ: an independent short-film maker and I do stories that compel their audiences to be interested in joining a movement. People will ask and say who is TheFanNJ: well he is a political pundit / social justice advocate, always running for office and writing short-films about the political endeavors of TheFanNJ.

As I watched and investigated this fast growing movement, which sprung from Media Attention: Occupy Wall Street, and the more famous slogan; "We are the 99%, (Join Us): You are the 99% (Join Us)." I didn't know about the people creating such a stir in politics. I first learned about this on a social networking site. And how they were organizing a massive protest – as I applauded them for trying, and completely forgot about them while creating a problem in New Jersey's politics.

Then an amazing thing happened, over 10,000 people managed to come together and protest against the corruption on Wall Street. And created the symbol of 1% and 99% -- where they were mad at the big banks, and their control over wealth, and wealth redistribution. As I saw these movements grow over the internet, and in the realms of media with: CNN, and Fox News, and the message that was being portrayed. I had to see what this movement was about, and I had to make it something big, and more meaningful than before. Plus, make sure that the right message was displayed, and not a centric view of radical students, who may be labeled as outlaws, or criminals. Okay, how did we get here: CEO of Chase Bank, and the CEO of Bank of America – wanted to increase their profit outlook, by increasing the service fees on those whom had bank accounts?

These fees would include a transaction fee on debt cards, and raise it to quarterly amount, or a transaction of $5, every-time you use the card. This created a rally and calling from a non-profit organization, where they created a fight. The first rally was on September 17, 2011 – where many people were arrested in a peaceful protest. The organization later became a household name that will be remembered in history as: Occupy Wall Street. In downtown Manhattan, in a place called: Zuccotti Park, 100 people made a tent and camped out in the park. They wanted to start a revolution, and had a clear message about what they saw – or what was happening with the big banks.

End Script:

What is the meaning of Occupy Wall Street: in letters and flyers posted, this movement is made up of separate organizations, with the right to organize: there were trade unions, unions, labor organizations, advocacy groups, and independent news organization?

Some of the letters and statements coming from this massive collection of people were written in these phases. Look and read the stories of America's left behind or forgotten culture. These letters are in no particular order—just research and developed.

October 20, 2011

Letter: Statement by the League of the Revolutionary Party.

A chance to start a working-class Fightback –

On October 19, the Delegates Meeting of the New York Central Labor Council (CLC) voted unanimously for New York's unions to mobilize for a massive march on Wall Street on November 5, 2011. The power to act on the delegates' vote now lies with the CLC Executive Board, which is composed of the city's local union presidents.

The CLC brings together delegates from the AFL-CIO and other unions in New York City. If its major unions make a serious effort to mobilize their members, we could see a truly massive march on Wall Street that challenges the ongoing efforts to make working-class and poor people pay the price for the economic crisis.

The motion to March

Moved by AFM Local 802 Recording Vice President John O'Connor and seconded by TWU Local 100 Vice President for RTO Kevin Harrington as well as other delegates, the motion concluded:

1. This body call on its member unions as well as other unions and community organizations to build a massive march on Wall Street of hundreds of thousands, mobilizing organized and unorganized workers, on November 5, 2011the first Saturday of the month;

2. That this protest demands that can unite all workers, poor people and all those facing the brunt of the crisis:
   Working People Shouldn't Pay for a Crisis That They Didn't Make!
   No to Layoffs, Budget and Service Cuts!

Create Jobs, Build Infrastructure with a Federal Program of Public Works!
Stop Police Harassment of the Wall Street Occupation!

3. And to this end, we appeal to other unions bodies, council and federations around the country to organize similar protest actions across the country on November 5, 2011.

The idea for the march and motion to the CLC was initiated by transit, janitorial, city and college worker union members and young Wall Street Protesters who are supporters of the League for the Revolutionary Party. Abig boost for the motion came when an LRP supporter raised the motion at a meeting of the City College Chapter of PSC union and it was overwhelmingly approved. A petition backing the motion quickly gained the support of other trade unionists and a large number of Wall Street occupiers and protesters, a good number of whom attended the CLC meeting to distribute the motion and speak in favor of it.

The Challenge Before Us

The Challenge now is to make sure that the union leaders respect the CLC delegates' vote and really build the march. That won't be easy

Since the economic crisis broke out on Wall Street in 2008, this country's union leaders have barely lifted a finger tin opposition to the wasting of trillions of taxpayers' dollars on bailing out the banks and the terrible wave of layoffs and budget cuts that have followed. Comfortable in their positions of privilege, the union leaders have mostly been concerned with holding onto their power and channeling workers' anger into the trap of voting for the Democratic Party.

Signs Of Blackslinding

In the CLC Delegates Meeting itself, there were already signs of backsliding. No sooner was the vote being taken than CLC President Vincent Alvarez, while promising to respect the decision, seemed to suggest that the CLC Executive Board might need to be flexible about some of the details of the protest. Any union leader who takes a real step toward organizing struggles by workers against the attacks on the jobs and living standards will find us and many militant workers ready to join them in that effort. But in our experience, the pro-capitalist, pro-democratic Party union leaders can be expected to use an inch of "Flexibility" to avoid organizing a real fightback against the anti-worker attacks.

Mass Worker's Struggle Is Needed

In fact the way today's union leaders avoid organizing struggles by their own members, let alone in conjunction with militant young people like those participating in the Wall Street occupation, came through in the discussion of other topics of that meeting. For example, regarding the struggle going to vote down Ohio Governor Kasich's vicious union-busting laws, a report was given describing the unions' almost total reliance on phone-banking and door-knocking and very little on mass worker rallies, let alone strikes. But all experiences teaches that to defend their rights, jobs and living standards, workers can only afford to rely on their own power to unite in the struggle. In Wisconsin an occupation of the Capital Building and massive protests against Republican Governor Scott Walker's union-busting legislation led to growing calls for a general strike. But union leaders wasted that momentum and channeled the struggle into a passive election campaign that was predictably defeated.

Build The Movement

So we must make every effort to build further support for the march and to make sure that the city's union leaders make it happen. Union members should take every opportunity to challenge their representatives, from Shop Stewards to elected office holders, to make sure their unions dues does everything it can build for the march. Motions in support of the march should be raised in every possible union meeting. Organizations and individuals, who haven't already endorsed the march should be encouraged to do so by, writing to:

workersmarchagainstwallstreet@gmail.com .

Beware of Tokenism

Importantly, we must watch out for and denounce any tokenism or lip-service from the union leaders. The unions can send organizations all over to rally support for the march. They can print and distribute leaflets, record and broadcast video and radio messages, to build a mighty protest. That's the sort of real mobilization we need. The widespread support for the Wall Street protests shows that workers' bitter sense of injustice is turning toward a recognition of the need for action. This is an important chance to take forward the fightback against the capitalist' attacks that is so long overdue.

For more information contact the LRP!

The League for the Revolutionary Party (LRP) is a revolutionary organization of workers and youth. With co-thinkers around the world in the Communist Organization for the Fourth International (COFI), we work to build an international party to lead the struggle to overthrow capitalism. For more information, contact: **LRP, P.O. Box 1936, Murry Hill Station, New York, NY 10156: Phone 212-330-9017**
Email: *irpcofi@earthlink.net* :
website: *www.lrp-cofi.org*

This was one of the letters that was written about this great movement. And how many different organizations came together in support of the Wall Street Movement, and who is behind the movement. And when taking a trip down to the park in New York City, you will find some interesting events going on, and some interesting things happening. The mission about Occupy Wall Street became the individual stories and life of humans harmed by the banking industry – or what we call the financial sector.

People largely noted that the number one case of reasoning for them to be in solidarity with protesting citizens was: Chase Bank, Bank of America, and the rest of the top five banks. Yet, they were extremely hard pressed by Bank of America's scheme on derivatives, and mortgages.

What this movement means to those trying to send a message to the establishment is something that is bigger than the two? And this letter next shows the declaration of Occupy Wall Street. This small community even addressed some of the basic issues by drafting a letter of declaring their vow and organizational rights.

Declaration of the Occupation of New York City[1]

This document was accepted by the NYC General Assembly
on September 29, 2011
Translations: French, Slovak, Spanish, German, Italian, Arabic, Po
rtuguese

As we gather together in solidarity to express a feeling of mass injustice, we must not lose sight of what brought us together. We write so that all people who feel wronged by the corporate forces of the world can know that we are your allies.

As one people, united, we acknowledge the reality: that the future of the human race requires the cooperation of its members; that our system must protect our rights, and upon corruption of that system, it is up to the individuals to protect their own rights, and those of their neighbors; that a democratic government derives its just power from the people, but corporations do not seek consent to extract wealth from the people and the Earth; and that no true democracy is attainable when the process is determined by economic power. We come to you at a time when corporations, which place profit over people, self-interest over justice, and oppression over equality, run our governments. We have peaceably assembled here, as is our right, to let these facts be known.

- They have taken our houses through an illegal foreclosure process, despite not having the original mortgage.

---

[1] http://www.nycga.net/resources/declaration/

Occupy Wall Street: Letters from Wall Street Protesters

- They have taken bailouts from taxpayers with impunity, and continue to give Executives exorbitant bonuses.
- They have perpetuated inequality and discrimination in the workplace based on age, the color of one's skin, sex, gender identity and sexual orientation.
- They have poisoned the food supply through negligence, and undermined the farming system through monopolization.
- They have profited off of the torture, confinement, and cruel treatment of countless animals, and actively hide these practices.
- They have continuously sought to strip employees of the right to negotiate for better pay and safer working conditions.
- They have held students hostage with tens of thousands of dollars of debt on education, which is itself a human right.
- They have consistently outsourced labor and used that outsourcing as leverage to cut workers' healthcare and pay.
- They have influenced the courts to achieve the same rights as people, with none of the culpability or responsibility.
- They have spent millions of dollars on legal teams that look for ways to get them out of contracts in regards to health insurance.
- They have sold our privacy as a commodity.
- They have used the military and police force to prevent freedom of the press.
- They have deliberately declined to recall faulty products endangering lives in pursuit of profit.
- They determine economic policy, despite the catastrophic failures their policies have produced and continue to produce.
- They have donated large sums of money to politicians, who are responsible for regulating them.
- They continue to block alternate forms of energy to keep us dependent on oil.

- They continue to block generic forms of medicine that could save people's lives or provide relief in order to protect investments that have already turned a substantial profit.
- They have purposely covered up oil spills, accidents, faulty bookkeeping, and inactive ingredients in pursuit of profit.
- They purposefully keep people misinformed and fearful through their control of the media.
- They have accepted private contracts to murder prisoners even when presented with serious doubts about their guilt.
- They have perpetuated colonialism at home and abroad.
- They have participated in the torture and murder of innocent civilians overseas.
- They continue to create weapons of mass destruction in order to receive government contracts.*

To the people of the world,

We, the New York City General Assembly occupying Wall Street in Liberty Square, urge you to assert your power.

Exercise your right to peaceably assemble; occupy public space; create a process to address the problems we face, and generate solutions accessible to everyone.

To all communities that take action and form groups in the spirit of direct democracy, we offer support, documentation, and all of the resources at our disposal.

Join us and make your voices heard!

The movement began to spread, and notary began to emerge. As the occupants in Zuccotti Park began to have their voices heard. I encouraged the protestors at home, and helped organize people to their rallies from the bench. Yet, I needed to see their stories, since we all shared the same common goals: which was economic equality. So on one of my mission and explorations on entering this well designed movement lead me to see Jeffery Sach. Jeffery Sach, was a lobbyist that donated and campaigned for Senator Barack Obama – while helping his organization gain millions in government subsidies.

Scene 2: Celebs at Occupy Wall Street
Narrator:
After getting invitation on an invite to come down to Zuccotti Park, and view those that were affected by the economic crisis and are protesting about the Wall Street benefits. I got my first glimpse of those that were harmed in the process. It was shocking for me to see that there was a large amount of people—harmed and looking at the problems of the 99%. Like, a major problem with Chase Bank: one of the major problems the signs shown—where: how military families where harmed with refinancing loans on mortgages. Like soldiers would take three or more tours to fight for this country overseas, and come home to an overdue principal on their mortgages. And when they couldn't refinance those debts, it went into default.

I then walked upon a conversation being held by Jeffery Sachs, although I couldn't hear the conversation that he was chanting out to the people. Yet, the bulk of his conversation was about: how the upper 1% or the super rich became – super rich. And how the policy makers where tilted too become even more wealthy under the current system. The conversation started out as, the wealthy are getting to much leverage and too much control on the policy makers.

And even though President Barack Obama has been trying to legislate for the middle class, he still has meetings with the super rich. And right now, President Barack Obama is having a $5,000 per plate fundraiser with some of the big bankers that are swaying votes. Jeffery Sach, latter complained about how campaigns were financed, and would like to see a different type of leadership. He also was weary about Barack Obama's pledge to raise $1 billion dollars, and how Karl Rove made a pledge to match that with $1 billion of his own raised. As he complained that with all of this amount of money being raised, we can place that as a down-payment for our national dept.

-------- End Script --------

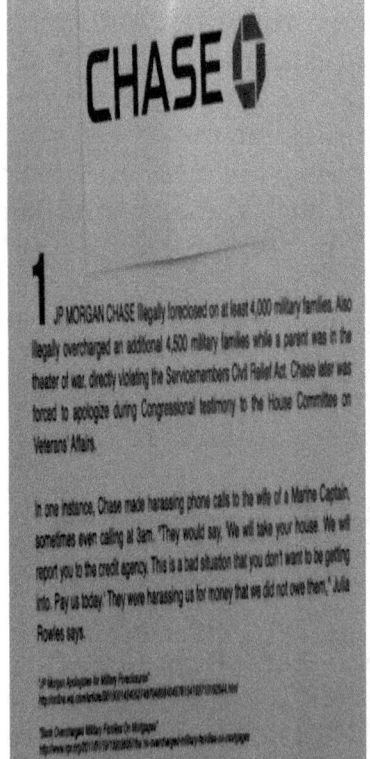

Many times we as people lose focus on what is happening in our surroundings, and we tend to take our minds off the bigger picture. And this movement that has scoped a nation, wants their voice and perception heard.

And that is what drawn me to this movement, and why their story should be told.

Picture by Omar Dyer: Copyrights ©2010 Coaches! 101

Some people believe that the clock is ticking on the government to take action on addressing the concerns of the people that are: "Are the 99%." And since the movement isn't going anywhere and people are gearing up to make a solid stand—more and more people are joining the movement that helps groom something big.

And my view and job is to make sure the right message about what is going on with those that occupy Wall Street – get across. And that the agenda, is clear: where if leaders are about to groom and grow. That they (leadership), understand the obligations to those who are in the 99% on economic equality: and to know that the people who are protesting aren't a bunch of angry people, or criminals—mist fist, or outsiders, and that they are real people with real problems. On how these problems that have come about with greed, and allowing the corruption portion to affect the politics in economics; where it leads to poverty in this country.

When we talk about the demonstrations happening in this country about those—whom have become victims of a corporation wilt on greed? When you have over-whelming disproportionate levels of economic wealth, and a system defending the upper class? You will get and have a second world of people protesting and expressing their rights in the streets.

Yet, during these protest you see people handing out flyers, and organizations counter-acting as one. And the focus point was to get the message out about corporate greed / plus economic equality. A lot of people involved in this movement have been affected by the rising and growing concerns of what is going on at: Wall Street. Even Celebrities have made sound bites, and marches with those that represent the people who are part of the 99%.

Scene three Micheal Moore:

Narrator:

When Micheal Moore brought Russell Simmons to Zuccotti Park, people crowed the park to take pictures, and listen to what he had to say? And majority of his complaints where about corporate greed and control of who has the wealth in this country! CNN which is a news broadcasting center – came in droves, and supported the movement in a vast majority of timing and space. CNN's presence made this movement a one-sided view: of an angry mob of people, occupying a public / private park in New York City right next to Wall Street. And right at that moment the perception of Occupy Wall Street was created.

And then people started appearing at this park to see and speculate on what is going on, plus show support or now about the problems that they face with those who are calling themselves: "The 99%."

A closer look at some of the people protesting in Zuccotti Park, New York City like:

Jed Brandt, is an editor of the Occupied Wall Street Journal, and founding participant in the Kasama Project. This is the newspaper that brings the latest events happening in the small community growing inside a city. The Occupied Wall Street Journal written by those who occupy this park – brings a story of a story for those that are occupants.

Eric Ribellarsi: is the national organizer of the Kasama Project, recently returned from deep investigations into the "movement of the squares," in Greece and the revolutionary movement in Nepal.

Mike Ely: is a veteran revolutionary whose political life started with the early SDS and the Black Panther Party in the 1960's and covers decades of experience attempting to build revolutionary organizations, including among coal miners in the wildcat strike movement of the 1970's.

Organized by the Kasama Project – a communist effort to re-imagine and regroup for revolution in the U.S. All have been active in the Occupy Together movement in different cities.

Does this mean that communist are trying to mock or minimize the central government system? No, it means that the wealth of the country has brought those with different minds and agendas, on becoming more focused on one goal: Occupy Together for economic equality.

Yet, you can come to your own conclusions by visiting kasamaproject.org.

The movement is made up of good intentions to people talking about the underlining issues. And major reason why people are flocking to the occupy movement is based on the social impacts that has been structured without economic diversity. And the chances of this happening would mean a cultural shift, and compensation structure of those who occupy the term 1%. And what this meant for the people that had major economic concerns with their futures. A future where the rich has gotten richer, while the poor / homeless have gotten worse, and America: "which is called the land of opportunity – plus the creator of prosperity?" Has almost 11 million people living in poverty, and 8 million in prison – with 4 million on the board line!

A lot of people would like to know -- "what was the leading cause of the people rallying against the government they hold?" In 2010, Congress went into a more exclusive role of cuts, cuts, and cuts only approach. Where their approach was taking a magical number out of the budget and cutting it significantly? The Congress then passed a bill that included what people now call: The Paul Ryan Budget Plan. This plan eliminated programs that were essential to the growth of the country. And they did this without asking or taking an inquiry on the programs that they are cutting. They didn't make a choice based on the implications on how many jobs were affiliated to these programs. And as people took to the streets and protested Economic Equality, in New York City many of those ran into resistance. That resistance was called: Mayor Mike Bloomberg and Police Commissioner Ray Kelly.

And this mounted an extensive battle with protestors, and the uniformed men hired to protect them. The first contact wasn't televised but the national audience watch what happened on social networking sites—such as Facebook. Even though Facebook, was one of the major tools in incorporating the information, about the events taken place. It was the independent journalist, and others that kept media pressure on what was going on in the park.

The next action was to march on the Brooklyn Bridge, and as protesters took to the streets. They were confronted by the New York City Police. As the protesters were marching across the bridge, they were obeying the laws, by marching on the side walk. When the police tried to stop the protesters from marching across? That's when problems started to commerce. And at first people sat down, and assembled wanting to be arrested. Then other protesters took the streets and started to march in the streets of the bridge. Which then shut down the traffic going on the bridge and coming off the bridge?

Narrator:

The protesters took the Brooklyn Bridge protesting Mike Bloomberg, and how he tried to remove protestors from occupying Zuccotti Park. This lead to a major rally with the unions and other trade organizations – having a symbolic march on the Brooklyn Bridge, to tell the Mayor how they felt! The images showed captured the story of how a mayor and the police commissioner are violating the peoples' right to assemble. There was a clash with the police, a fight has come about, and the news didn't tell the real story of why such people are protesting in the streets.

End narration:

That led to a major outbreak and class with those who consider themselves apart of the 99%. The major reason why people are frustrated with the system is the level of patronage – plus the economic disparity for those that are a part of the 99%. Groups like Move-on.org played a major part of creating what this movement is about: and how people are mad as hell and will not take it anymore.

People would or wanted to know where and what was the beginning stage on why this movement became such a promising movement. Since the movement was suppose to be short term, and hit targets of corporate greed. Organizations mad at the notion and facts that they are being targeted and threaten by a massive movement to undermine the poor. Became the single calling for unions, trade organizations, and out labor protectors: believed in that their of fare wages. What placed this into motion was the massive protest to protect unions – where the governor of Wisconsin shoved through an amendment? The amendment that was passed in Wisconsin would have changed the collective bargaining rights for those that are public employees and are in the middle class. And the people united to shut down the government temporarily on a protest – that was union organized and very peaceful.

Wisconsin's Governor Scott Walker, made a political move that he may regret. When he signed into law, a bill that would put an end to collective bargaining rights? Trade organizations that where more about grass-rooting from an online perspective: where it brought out massive members of people to a cause. What made some dents into the growth on how online grass-root organizing was becoming the wave of the future? When progressive change, and bold progressive – helped organize people to join the protestors during the Occupy Wall Street Movement!

What that meant was at any moment around 10,000 people can roam the streets, and protest – organize, and practice their first amendment rights? This brought a level of security and awareness to this cause that has many people in the OWS (Occupy Wall Street): calling for serious discussions on economic equality. And lots of people had different reasons on why they are joining the movement – where many of those concerns, flowed in the direction of economic equality. Where the lives of the many are shared, and the views in disparity is equal?

Chapter 2:

Occupy Together

The perception on what is going on with the members who have taken up stock to occupy the streets. Have turned to the wrong direction in the light of the media, and of course people have a different agenda on why they occupy. Yet, the full and clear mission is to ensure that people have rights that are respected, and have a system where the economics of the country isn't tilted to those who are in the upper chills in wealth. Sure the problem may range in a fiscal direction on rules and regulations. In this movement you have many faces like: Anarchist. People who believe that there shouldn't be one rule of order for the people.

I spoke to one of the members of Occupy Wall Street occupation. One he's a student, and a young man – who happens to be in Theater Arts. His passion for arts, doesn't pay the bills when it comes to owning a mortgage, and rent for an apartment. And his idea of working some job that doesn't pay well – plus he would have to follow tough company rules – or abide by entitlement laws, that prevent him from engaging in drama. And since you can't find a money figure on currency for people like him: they generally believe that government must just get out of their way, and allow them to live off the fruits of the land.

To them it's more about the principal of a live of free will, and not the burdens placed on you with a live of corporate shills. And his life has been impacted by the singular principal for economic equality. The type of equality that would result a respect for the will of art! And I suddenly saw what he meant, and it wasn't that he was against government – he was against prevention. He is against the government preventing him from living the life he chooses, and not force him or others like him to live in a life on consumption of materials, and money.

And others like him had that same feeling that on where they no-longer trust government. No longer trust that corporations or the people that run them can or should be in control of how they consume their lives. People are frustrated that the government is centralized around the baring of what a corporation says, and how government compensates corporations; to provide living standards on which many of them don't generally agree to: but they must in order to buy an imprint on the life—that these same corporations promote. Whereas a lot of them don't want to place an imprinted face on and live in a system that drags your emotions down—to a point where the life you generally live; doesn't circumvent the life you choose to live! They wouldn't mind working for a company that allows them to practice their passions. Or live in a government that respects their rights to live and abide by those same passions of free will.

And after listening to this one young man's perspective, and his unfiltered hatred for how corporations control people's lives: plus don't allow them to live off the land and enjoy the lives they choose. Where he (or individuals like him) strongly believed that they should be in control of their lives: not to be a symbol for a way of life geared to those who own stock or shares in a system. Better to be known they didn't want to be systemized out of a life that enjoys, the sun – stars, moons, and people around them. Would you call them separatist or would you call them outlaws, criminals, or faceless creeds trying to destroy the fabrics of a centralized system based on the following of a material substance, on which has become a fabric more worshiped than the creator of the earth? No I wouldn't give this group of people a label like that, and there are some out there in which they persist on calling a group of people: in this manner—a cult. Would I call that group in this manner a Cult? No, I generally wouldn't label them a Cult either.

Even though many of them believes in the principles that God is the creator of life, and free will is the process that we must go through in order to a live we have chosen. As the reason for this movement to come together has formed from stories of a lot of people having problems on who and what controls the obligations—on the lives people live, and how they live that life. As a writer and a novelist, you must incorporate yourself with any movement. You must learn from those that are having hardships. And the hardships some of these members are having – have more to do with the patterns of how we live our full lives based on economics. Where the structure of our economic system is geared to protecting a central establishment? Or the perception that this establishment has on the leaders of our country! And brings the discussion to the notion of: what is the true meaning of life equality.

And should you sell your principles and passions in your choices – to live in a world of entitlements, and elitist. And a world without an emotion for life, respect for the opinions of others – plus the pursuit to happiness, as a chosen life anyone would like to live. Where a lot of them (OWS) believed in the movement as a monumental calling from two worlds inside one world right here on Earth? They want to live in a world where free will is at the table, and people are respected for how they chose to live their lives. When the mention of art becomes the life of the chosen?

The movement isn't a cult – more than a gathering of artist stuck in a system of corporate greed, with the lack of respect to those who choose to love their art. It's a student gathering for those who have mounted debt, and can't pay off with the salaries that they are currently living under— thus becoming a slave to an economic structure. It people being abused by the corporate system of structured bailouts, and people generated sell outs: since a bank can write off bad debts, while a person can't.

And banks aren't writing off bad debts to help those that purchased those debts – they are writing off these debts, for the banks own profit. I did speak of this in 2010 – when writing letters to Congress, and one of the letters marked!

The article, was called: New Economic Concerns; which was created to warn the members of Congress, about the five largest Banks: Bank of America, Chase Bank, Wells Fargo, Citi-Group, and Morgan Stangley.

September 2010:

Dear Members of Congress:

New Economic Concerns!

The problem we face on with how banks are treating minority businesses—low market, and shared dividends. With the $700 billion and $3 trillion in moneys passed by congress to get banks on board with the American Recovery Efforts—has turned south. That's the premature news on this economic shell that we can break: but fear, greed and lack of knowledge in the evaluation on business proceedings has continued a log jam in lending. The largest banks in the industry has been lying, and commencing heavy restrictions in how banks are treating those that bailed them out. Right now interest rates on the dollar are at bargaining prices—meaning banks are getting first cracks at low market moneys—where they're in turned into substantial profits undermining the need for recovery. Even though this industry had one of the largest years in 50 years: they've been ignorant and malicious to the malignant concerns of economic growth of this country! Meaning the respectful practices of those wanting to get into business— understand the taking plus makings of the financial structure. That's what T.A.R.P. was meant to do: Troubled Assets Relieve Program was meant to relieve assets from troubled companies in order to create growth in job creation.

What Happened: Banks took T.A.R.P. moneys ignored the practices of business, and resorted to business as usual? And as long as they fulfilled the guidelines on business practices that created the bubble we are placed in—the systematic problem hasn't been fixed or cured. The problem has been avoided, ignored and moved out. The future of America placed trust into the current banking system. And now it's time for banks to walk into that process of honoring contracts, future dividends and retail shares on online exchanges and future projections.

And not the practices of the pass—since it was lack of respect to fiscal scores or future yearly fiscal scores— turned the mess on economic stability into a systematic problem, only creates a quarterly problem at the beginning of each quarter. Problems that can be solved by helping small businesses—on getting profits sealed before the quarter starts to prevent problems at the end of a quarter. We just can't push this down to the side and make claims about books not being balanced. That's being afraid of working and making change come about—if we are afraid to recognize or reconcile the notion that business is changing, and online contracts, trading shares or on-demand goods, is now the new business tool for online companies.

On Demand goods are contracts that have waving futuristic prices. Meaning an investor would need to establish a financial history, whether positive or negative in order to conduct business with the bank! Then establish a line of credit (Banks) while creating a base to continue growth. It's a three system process on the boarding chips of business. While managing the production process to hold down employment to manage the goods on demand—as if there're interests in getting goods into the eyes of the consumer?

Let's say you have a great product: The Next Generation of Leaders. And let's say you have a creditable consumer base, where it leaves you with products waiting to be consumed—yet, the problem consists with assets and its protection. Meaning banks are picking and choosing what companies or what person they want to help.

After writing that article many people started to draft petitions to break up the big banks, and complain about the system of how the banks are getting more bucks, with less to bargain with. And at the same time during these same financial times – congress was passing more laws to restrict the lives of those affected in this economic crisis. And when Shelley Berkley (D) Nevada, Carol Shea-Porter (D) New Hampshire, David Dreier (R) California, Martin Heinrich (D) New Mexico, Sam Johnson (D) Texas, wrote and passed: HR 4061: Federal cyber Security Research. Which was supposed to help the system or government monitor cyber bullying? And during the tri-season after the bill was passed into law – state hoods have abused this agenda, and illegally monitored people. Giving technical contracts to companies, which monitored and recorded information of those in the state? Where that move gave more power to the states on infringing the lives of their residents without them evening knowing them?

As referencing to what that amendment is doing to the citizens of today: well, a bank can use that information from a monitoring committee—without your permission, and peak into a history that was normally forbidden, without this amendment! So if you have a history of an unbalance structured of debt, or have an account on social networking sites—some corporations where using that information to way in factors on hiring practices. And that meant, the hiring of a small business – since a loan coming from a 7(a) loan meant that the bank hired your business. Yet that didn't stop the banks from screwing the system, or the people – since banks where getting funds from the Internal Revenue Service: where the TEBs where at the rate of zero.

And to give you more information on what a TEB is: it's called Tax Exempt Bonds – which are normally for organizations that are in the financial sector, and are exempt from taxes. They are allowed to purchase these bonds, and resell them to consumers. The intention for these bonds where to spur consumer confidence. And the most a bank or a person can apply for in these bonds were $10,000—which by the way was called Surety Bonds. Surety Bonds are 100% money back bonds for banks and financial firms to purchase, so they can lend to consumer; thus spurring the economic growth. And when President Barack Obama, signed into law the Hire Act: which gave banks $33 billion in tax credits for the terms of a bond. Some banks used those short term credits, to buy out community banks. And to buy off capital gains of the top 1% who own direct exchanges in their market. What we would call, indirect trading—which would be speculative trading based on asset value, and assessment to market growth?

And what has been noted is that many banks were doing or practicing these practices. One to reap in profits from every source possible—while charging outrageous principals on interest rates for bonds given or sold. The people in charge of these practices by the banks were made profits off of a loophole in the tax code: where capital gains or interest rate stipends wasn't regulated or payable to the federal government. Yet, with all of this uncertainty –why has this movement come to the forefront. The movement to bring economic equality to America is long overdue—whereas a lot of people are saying; this is the time for the movement. People have become increasingly upset about the proportionate levels of disparity going to those who (occupy) the one percent? They are concerned that working hard, achieving and becoming a part of the image portrayed as the American Dream—have become entangled in economic insecurity for those that occupy the 99%.

The term called 99% comes from those that are not super rich, and have to work ordinary jobs, low income – poor, homeless, and any other that's not in the financial world and make over a million bucks. Although some of those that occupy the 99% are millionaires—in terms of what they are incorporated to do, other than how they are incorporated. Technically, I have no idea who and why the term 99% was created, and I don't generally know what it truly stands for—or how it's genetics groomed behind the rights of being called: 99%. But what I do know is one thing, for you not to be in the 99% you have to been a person or entity that has made more than the standard living—in a 70% increase.

So how does this play with those from Occupy Wall Street? On Monday December 12, 2011 at 7:30 am – an event called D12: Occupy Strikes Sachs: Organizers mocked Goldman Sachs. Goldman Sachs: created this climate of economic shell out. These statements come from the words of Matt Taibbi written in 2010 on Goldman Sachs which is a financial firm. "The first thing you need to know about Goldman Sachs is that it's everywhere. The world's most powerful investment bank is a great vampire squid wrapped around the face of humanity, relentlessly jamming its blood funnel into anything that smells like money."

The protestors called Goldman Sachs a money sucking vampire squid. And they organized an event of the West Coast Ports Blockade. They made this event as D12: Occupy Strikes Sachs! In the movement to secure or talk about the substantial concerns with economics and people losing their homes on a mortgage scheme; some protesters and writers; that wrote on economic concerns wanted to address these core issues. The occupy movement will strike back after the coordinated national attack on the occupations with a coordinated port shut down targeting EGT and Goldman Sachs, two 1% organizations that have been busting longshoremen's and tuckers' unions and committing egregious tax fraud at West Coast shipping ports.

The international investment banking firm Goldman Sachs owns large shares of shipping and transportation companies, power companies, meat processing plants, military weapons suppliers, fast-food restaurants, oil refineries, for-profit colleges, casinos, healthcare businesses, internet shopping outlets, department stores, and beyond. By pushing disastrously risky loans on society and harvesting the profits from chain businesses and our national infrastructure, Goldman Sachs raked in over $39 billion in revenue in the fiscal year of 2010. Moreover, although Goldman Sachs has received more subsidies and bailout-related funds than any other investment bank, in 2009 the company awarded its senior employees $18 billion in bonuses, followed by $16 billion in bonuses in 2010 and $10 billion in bonuses in 2011. At the end of 2007, just on the brink of the bank's federal bailout, Goldman Sachs CEO Llyod Blankfein actually received a record-breaking mega-bonus of $67.9 million.

Many people started protesting about this and what they called a vampire squid – as I marched with the protestors that have occupied New York. They wanted the world to know the basic of what they are fighting for – plus the mission that they people are marching on. One of the major issues that brought chills down many people's spine is the singular notion that Goldman Sachs used its money, and power to strangle our government mechanisms as well—in 2010, Goldman Sachs spent $4.61 million on corporate lobbyist and spent $1,307,692 paying off politicians. In the words of journalist Chris Hedges, "there's no way within the corporate state to vote against the interest of Goldman Sachs."

From my perspective I wanted to stress that this information came from the New York General Assembly also known as Occupy Wall Street. And known that many of the CEOs from Goldman Sachs were charged by the SEC!

The movement became something that nobody could have predicted. And as the protest increased, some of the ironies in the movement with those that are poor—have become a strange or tangled web. Some people in the movement think that getting arrested is the best form or way to get that message across. Where getting arrested became more important than sending and spreading the message?

I myself was becoming more and more attached to what people called Occupied Wall Street. Because I believed that where the foot soldiers, to spoke up for what I have been talking about for years. And finally someone is listening—yet, I didn't know: this movement was going to be another way for congress to suppress, my voice. When I joined this movement, it was all about occupying the neighborhoods, and streets – occupying the world and freeing the people from the abuse of government. People were tired of their government, and those in charge that they wanted to take it back. I joined the movement because I needed a place to go and vent my frustrations with how this economy has change. And how everything has become so polarized, where everything became or gave an impression of being corrupted! What saddened me is the notion that elected leaders took great pride – in the kill the opposition movement—where the word compromise became such a hated word. Or how the job creators where being script from that moment to create jobs! Also, how discriminative elected leaders have gotten towards: in my opinion, me.

They wanted to send the Obama administration a clear message, and I guess I was the fall guy. The target that the message would be sent to and on – or at least it was the company I represented. Since my image and pen-name placed Senator Barack Obama into the White House; someone had to pay the price. And there were some that wanted to make and break a clear message.

This is why I joined Occupy Wall Street, not because I needed a lift in fame. I could care less about the fame, not because I wasn't to be in the spotlight. I joined and teamed up with them because – government has turned a blind eye on the people. Just look and listen to their stories, some of the stories – are repeats of what I have been writing about, way before the general public and media, start noticing the problem. I joined because I had a whole year in fighting with Bank of America, on their loan fraud. Where the judges, stated my information would and could bring indictments on people, since this was a crime to place people in this type of harm. And you want to know the reason why a judge in Hudson County New Jersey, turned a cheek. Because of the rules for representation without a legal representative: Meaning, many judges were favoring attorney's that took the bar, and believed in their practice.

To this day, I will always say: Presslyer and Presslyer Law Firm—are a bunch of crooks, with a law specialist license. And I will not pay them for the fraud that was created, and that firm has a long list of complaints. The movement isn't about Omar Dyer, or the problems that I may face. This movement is about showing light to the unjust ways of how government or leaders in government are harming the system. In 2010, a Tea-Party led Republican congress—leading the party were Neo-Conservatives like Scott Garrett (5 terms) as a congressman. He drafted an amendment called H.R. 4884. Which is known as: `**United States Covered Bond Act of 2010**'? H.R. 4884 does is allows certain business the ability to structure bonds. And it allowed some banks, or what the people called, blood sucking squids (Goldman Sachs) to gain information for the interested public—bond off those goods, and sell them in an overseas market. This made the amount because of the notion that it was ANCILLARY ASSET.

ANCILLARY ASSET- The term `ancillary asset' means, with respect to any cover pool—any interest rate or currency swap associated with any eligible asset, substitute asset, or other ancillary asset in the cover pool; any credit enhancement or liquidity arrangement associated with any eligible asset, substitute asset, or other ancillary asset in the cover pool; any guarantee, letter-of-credit right, or other secondary obligation that supports any payment or performance on an eligible asset, substitute asset, or other ancillary asset in the cover pool; and any proceeds of, or other property incident to, any eligible asset, substitute asset, or other ancillary asset in the cover pool.

You're thinking and saying – how did this change the game for Goldman Sachs. Well, by using Community Block Grants, and partnering with investors, Goldman Sachs: 1000 small business initiative was able to buy up or gain assets from consumers (legal), use that investment to write off the cost (legal) and mark down bonds to spur growth, with public money. It allowed them to get interest free exempt bonds, where they were allowed to set their own rates, and sell them off.

What made this a major problem, is when Congress – tried to pick and choose, which business can benefit from this and what business, can't? Buy creating this, and then going after people, who benefited from the investment—while allowing five companies seal the bond rating market made this a major problem. Since they were using a method of block and stall, and while they allowed Hedge-fund managers, municipal bonds, and insurance bookers; on having troubles, with cashing in on bonds—even though, they fully qualified, under the terms of the amendment placed forth. And buy Congress, force feeding credits, tax credits, and bonds—with strict rules set by the states. A state can deliberately hold, disburse, or reallocate those funds, without the cost or gained assets effecting the operations of government. Small talk, Goldman invested in the people, and government changed the rules at the local level.

States were making budget cuts, when private sector growth was growing. Like, firing public employees just so that the economy would stagnant and fall flat! Creating a bubble within a bubble, that can easily be avoid – if congress / or the states met the obligations of the bonds that were structured, in the amendments that they passed. In any case, I wouldn't place the full blame on Goldman Sachs, for how the terms were met. Since they didn't write the federal rules, and didn't foresee the states contradicting the federal government. And what this has done was create a structure of uncontrollable money management—giving super cuts, for investments; and troubled buyout plans for consumers of the states. And when Congress broke the backs with their $1.3 trillion dollar budget cut, there was nothing written in the language that would say: what they are cutting. Thus, allowing the government on sending everything into a spiral spin, while creating economic uncertainty in the United States' economic exchange.

Where those who had the balance sheets to marginalize their assets for TEBs, weren't getting paid— since congress, (including the president) were delaying payments on bonds, already paid in full. And by congress delaying the payments of one bond holder; sent the rest of the market into an ever going cycle of untruth in the bonding industry, plus the taxing code. Since there is no reason to hold up the payment, place a stop on the process—or even block the process. And a lot of people including the super rich that already paid for the release of the bond are wondering; why those in congress are playing political games. When it was noted that they are doing so to send a clear message on –one single consumers' (paid for) assets? Congress, wanted to embarrass the president, and make democrats take the fall for everything wrong with government. And in my best opinion, this is why people are protesting on the streets, in this occupied movement. They are wondering what is the hold up—how is congress going to place a control on the economy, plus stop the bleeding when it comes to the rich becoming super-rich, and the middle-class becoming low-income to poor; or the increasing numbers of those in poverty. Plus, they wanted to know, where the jobs are or why can't leaders find creditable solutions on creating jobs. And to make sure that states and local government assemblies follow the agenda of the federal government.

As many people would know, these are made in good intentions. Yet, you can't favor one level of the economy and block plus ban everyone else. And when you have one vampire reap in profits—you will get another. Yet, Chase Bank started this fight years before Goldman Sachs, made the move forward. And Chase Bank waited until a Goldman Sachs type of firm made the move before they followed behind. And what made it worse, was the schemes brought in by Chase Bank. They were marketing lottery games for their patrons; while extracting huge hidden fees.

People, (Chase Bank) have been ranting and displaying a practical view on my perceptions of Chase Bank. Since the bank hires a lot of people, and have become the way of life for those working in the bank. The practices of the bank, aren't new – they literally managed this shift to become a consumer of insider personal wealth. A letter written to board members on what they can use as leverage on exchanges outside of the company.

Chase Bank Memo

In addition, because the 401(k) Plan offers JPMC common stock as an investment option, pursuant to Section 306 of the Sarbanes-Oxley Act of 2002 JPMC directors and Section 16 officers are not permitted to trade in JPMC equity securities while 401(k) Plan participants are unable to transact in the 401(k) Plan. This means that except as provided in the next paragraph, during the blackout period you may not directly or indirectly purchase, sell, or otherwise acquire or transfer any JPMC equity securities (including the exercise of any options or the sale of any restricted stock). This prohibition applies to JPMC equity securities you hold both inside and outside the 401(k) Plan.

Gifts, dividend reinvestments under a dividend reinvestment plan and trading pursuant to a 10b5-1 trading plan are exempt from this prohibition.

Please note that the restrictions described in this notice are in addition to the normal restrictions on trading activity that JPMC imposes on directors and executive officers. In particular, you continue to be subject to the window period policy which prohibits most transactions until the next window period and to the pre-clearance requirements prior to any transaction in JPMC securities.

Anthony J. Horan, Corporate Secretary

JPMorgan Chase & Co.

The memo above was written in 2004, and this started a phase of uncontrolled trading—where the blackout periods started in 2007. What makes this a major problem, is some of those consumers who have purchased or invested in Chase Bank from 2008 until now are still in that "blackout period," Which means the underwriter of potential assets, can't get any bonuses—until the obligations of some securities have been restructured or met either (private / public) under the rules and regulations Sarbanes-Oxley Act of 2002. As, I have been saying from day one: Chase Bank took federal moneys to help the consumers with finances. Then, gave bonus checks to board members investing in the assets written off (insider trading) while lobbying congress, for better tax breaks; while some of their consumers were still in a blackout period.

Break it down, your hidden fees where paying for the retirement plans of employers of the bank, while the bank reaped in profits on federal compensation during backout periods from 2007-2010.

If you want more proof – here is the entire article from Craig Torres and Caroline Salas Gage. This article was written in the Bloomberg Report on September 28, 2011, and it takes about or summarized what I have been saying since 2004. The Federal Reserve, chastised by Congress for lending money to foreign institutions including a Libyan-owned bank, is once again the lender of last resort for banks around the world it knows little about. Three years after the collapse of Lehman Brothers Holdings Inc., money-market borrowing rates for dollars are rising, leading the Fed and European Central Bank to make the currency available to Europe's institutions for as many as three months. U.S. prime money-market funds cut their exposure to euro-zone Bank Deposits and commercial paper, or short-term IOUs, to $214 billion in August from $391 billion at the end of last year, according to JPMorgan Chase & Co. data.

The failure of regulators worldwide to address European banks' fragile dependence on short-term funding is "putting the Fed in a really awkward position," said Karen Shaw Petrou, managing partner at Federal Financial Analytics, a Washington regulatory research firm whose clients include the biggest U.S. banks. The swaps with Europe "are an extremely advantageous political football" for critics of the Fed, she said. The extended funding comes as the U.S. central bank is already under fire for its unprecedented monetary stimulus. Republican leaders including Representative John Boehner of Ohio and Senator Mitch McConnell of Kentucky wrote Chairman Ben S. Bernanke and the Board of Governors on Sept. 19, asking them to "resist further extraordinary intervention in the U.S. Economy."

Lawmaker Criticism

Representative Ron Paul, a Texas Republican who wants to abolish the Fed, and Senator Bernard Sanders, a Vermont independent, have criticized its loans to foreign institutions. "The Fed has made good on most of its investments over the years, but increasing its exposure and that of the U.S. government to foreign banks is a moral-hazard problem," said Edward Royce of California, the third most-senior Republican on the House Financial Services Committee. "We are effectively incentivizing U.S. money-market funds to continue to finance these banks." U.S. regulators also are becoming less patient with what are turning out to be dollar-funding runs against foreign banks. Financial institutions are too dependent on short-term money- market investors that tend "to flee at the first signs of distress," William C. Dudley, president of the Federal Reserve Bank of New York, said Sept. 23 in a Washington speech.

Regulators also lack access to data on foreign institutions operating in the U.S. that would allow them to "make informed judgments about the adequacy of such firms' capital and liquidity buffers," he said.

Large Losses

Investors are fleeing because of concern that banks will take large losses if a euro-zone nation such as Greece defaults. Europe's debt crisis has generated as much as 300 billion euros ($407 billion) in credit risk for the region's banks, the International Monetary Fund said last week. Against the euro, the dollar is heading for its biggest monthly advance since November last year as European policy makers fail to contain their region's sovereign-debt crisis. The euro traded at $1.3606 as of 1:25 p.m. today in New York.

The London Interbank Offered Rate at which banks say they can borrow for three months in dollars rose for a 14th day today to 0.36856 from 0.36522 percent yesterday, according to data from the British Bankers' Association. ECB Coordination The ECB said Sept. 15 it will coordinate with the Fed and other central banks to provide three-month dollar loans to banks to ensure they have enough of the currency through the end of the year. The Fed bears no foreign-exchange or credit risk on the swap lines because the Frankfurt-based ECB is its counterparty. There were $575 million in outstanding swaps with foreign central banks as of Sept. 21, Fed data show. The ECB loaned a similar amount of cash to two euro-area banks earlier this month in seven-day transactions. The first of three ECB three-month dollar-loan offers starts Oct. 12.

The Fed facility provides a critical "ceiling" on funding squeezes that allows investors to avoid panic and distinguish between healthy and troubled banks, said Jerome Schneider, head of the short-term strategies and money-markets desk at Pacific Investment Management Co. in Newport Beach, California. "What you don't want to have is liquidity risk become intertwined with solvency risk," Schneider said. The swap lines are "the foundation right now to provide a backstop."

Biggest Borrowers

After the criticism earlier this year of lending to overseas institutions -- including Arab Banking Corp., part-owned by the Central Bank of Libya, after Lehman collapsed in 2008 -- New York Fed researchers said U.S. branches of foreign banks were among the biggest borrowers from the discount window because they lack deposit bases. The window is the Fed's oldest backstop-lending tool. In an April 13 post on the New York bank's research blog, the researchers said these institutions have relied more heavily on so-called wholesale funding for dollars, including the money markets and foreign-exchange swaps. Supporting these banks helped maintain foreign investment in the U.S., they said. The Fed "does need to be concerned about how a liquidity run on the European banks will impact us -- our financial markets, our financial institutions, the economy as a whole," said Republican Representative Kevin Brady of Texas, the vice chairman of Congress's Joint Economic Committee. It needs to define its safety-net policies and use the extension of its credit as a lever to persuade European regulators to work on funding stability, he added. He will call on Bernanke to address these concerns at an Oct. 4 hearing, he said.

Policy Gap

"The Fed's lack of a lender-of-last-resort policy really does create tremendous market uncertainty" and provides an incentive for institutions "to run to the politicians," Brady said. "It does create moral hazard, no doubt about it." Euro-zone banks and other institutions were more than $350 billion in debt to the Fed's emergency-lending facilities at one point during the 2008-2009 financial crisis, according to datacompiled by Bloomberg News.

The analysis was based on Fed documents released earlier this year after court orders upheld Freedom of Information Act requests by Bloomberg LP, the parent company of Bloomberg News, and News Corp.'s Fox News Network LLC. Fed lending to these entities totaled more than $100 billion on an average day. Dexia SA (DEXB), based in Brussels and Paris, was the biggest euro-area borrower, with as much as $58.5 billion of Fed loans on Dec. 31, 2008. BNP Paribas (BNP) SA in Paris borrowed as much as $29.3 billion on April 18, 2008. The largest U.S. borrower, New York-based Morgan Stanley (MS), took $107.3 billion of loans on Sept. 29, 2008.

Unstable Funding

Banks that rely on unstable short-term funding risk having to return to official sources for money until liquidity and capital are bolstered, said Viral Acharya, a New York University Stern School of Business professor and author of books on financial stability. "All the national regulators have to agree that their banks need to raise capital," he said. "The regulators are not sufficiently united. No one country is taking the leadership to realize the problem is getting out of hand." The Basel committee said today it would speed up work on a minimum liquidity rule designed to make lenders more resistant to a short-term funding crunch. Work on "key areas" of the so- called liquidity-coverage ratio now will be completed "well in advance" of the original mid-2013 deadline, the committee said. The measure is scheduled to take effect in January 2015.

While the Fed is legally required to lend to banking entities in its districts, it "does have a choice" regarding how it will extend the swap lines, said William Poole, former president of the Federal Reserve Bank of St. Louis. "European governments have substantial dollar holdings of U.S. Treasury securities, so why not sell some of their dollar securities to support their own banks?"

So what the article is saying, or trying to convey are the real factors, on copying the model, created in America. A model, where they use tax bonds, to offset assets (not really sealing of the maturity) while charging fees, rates, and payment plans; then hiring people, and lobbying for more employment credits—just to marginalize a market. And their marketing scheme was to trick the consumers, into winning a lottery with these gimmicks, on what you can purchase. And these are some of the reasons why people are made at the banks. Yet, they should be made a the monitoring services, or congress for favoring one class of people, and not looking out for blood sucking money squids.

The five top banks in the world, abused the system designed to help all—and neo-conservatives in congress, placed politics and favors for those that are in the super rich category over the lives, of those that are considered low income; or under the poverty levels. While majority of this was done to send clear messages to: President Barack Obama, or some pledge made on a campaign trial to defund everything, overturn collective bargaining agreements, while killing the spending curve in America. Their cut taxes approach in Government, without any revenue sharing amendments, only played part in a offsetting the tax code.

And put majority of the people you see protesting in the streets—in the streets to protest, against government oppression. It started in the early summer—and popped its face in New York City. New York became the heart of the beast, the capital of where banks come to do business. Most of the top five banks have large establishments in New York City. And from here is where people started to occupy.

Chapter 3

Wall Street Occupied

One of the proudest moments in the movement to bring talks about social change—shown it's face with these protesters! I remember going to New York City, walking around near the World Trade Center site, and looking at how dull the area looked. Like there was no life, on expression—people were depressed, and times were stagnant. I said to myself, the people need to brighten this area up. Then it happened, a group of people, build a massive protest in what we called: Zuccotti Park. They came on the night of September 17, 2011; and rallied the world. I was shocked to know that this was actually happening, and how over 100 people started out in protesting in this park—as weeks come about, the few turned into the many; greatly done with the social media.

They marched all over the city, creating massive interruption to the system and the establishment. Plus mocked most of the times: Mayor Bloomberg. Then at the end of the week, we saw the first tent. Once New York allowed the first tent to become noticeable, many more tents came up—starting a wide-spreading massive movement for social justice. This was starting to turn and become an historical event. And they have rights to the movement—yet, what draw me in to the movement, is the single notion—that we (students) and advocates went down to Wall Street. And shut the place down for 12 minutes. People came in droves to be a part of the rally to shut down Wall Street. Why because Mayor Mike Bloomberg, made a bold move to invade the protesters' rights and tried to forcefully remove them from the park. Trade organizations, and unions rallied people to come down to the park and protect the people.

And in a bold strike back move, the leaders of OWS (Occupy Wall Street) organized a rally on Wall Street. On, September 30th 2011 – at 7:30am, we organized around 9,000 people, plus on-lookers to march three blocks down, to Wall Street.

As I was roaming the crowd, looking at the people in the square across the street from Zuccotti Park—all waiting for the word to, march down to the American Stock Exchange. The Leaders had to find a route that would allow the protesters, to get close or in front of the place. The goal was to shut it down, and shut down the traffic going in and around. So we all march seven blocks, until we found a spot on Wall Street and Beaver Street. We set up shop in front of two entry points: in front of Starbucks, and in front of Lens Craft. And we staged a human wall in front of police barricades. And the object was to stop workers and traders from getting to work on time, and shut down the stock exchange. As we rallied the street protesting what has happened at the hands of the big banks, we came together as a unit—on shutting down Wall Street.

The top organizer asked me to help organize the human wall in front of Starbuck. And for us to hold the position to get arrested, and we had 40 people holding the mount—while 15 were arrested. And on the other side of the block in front of the American Exchange building, we the protesters; closed down that side of the block. And to send a message to the police, a cardboard barricade was made to mock the police, as people who stood behind the barricade. In the middle of the street; where no traffic or movement was able to get by for 30 minutes! And once the four top leaders of the protest were arrested, people wanted to know or see how the movement was going to survive. And other organizers stepped forward, including myself and ranged more block to block protest.

And in the back of the American Exchange Building— man of the protestors, rallied a statement stand. As Mayor Bloomberg, and police commissioner Ray Kelly, came down to confront the protestors. They arrested the leader of the movement: her name wasn't told, but there was a small fight with Ray Kelly, and protestors protecting her.

After that small diplomatic exchange – some of the organizers made way to end this march: which was scheduled to end at 11:30am. Everyone came together and march our way back to the park—where there we saw the impact of the movement. There were more people in the park, than it was on Wall Street. Yet, that wasn't the end of the rally and fight. Since, we marched from Wall Street all the way up to Times Square, in a march for solidarity. We took the streets, in marching for—as we walked the streets. It was long and drenching, to walk almost half of the peninsula in New York City, to the major marking point: Times Square. And when we got there, after walking for far so long – I couldn't remember the time we reached Time Square, but taking 47th street right in front of Bank of America, the Time Square: Stage—plus on the block of TGIF restaurant, was something nobody has ever done.

We as a people, and team of protestors—took Time Square; were we shut down the entire block on 47th street. And what happened on that block will shock the world. It may not shock you or them now but when the time is right, and as the story unfolds; people will look at what happened on Wall Street—and then what went down in Time Square, New York; as the game changer for OWS. The police set up there large barricades because they knew that a crowd of people (protesting) were marching up 6th avenue going to Time Square, and we (the protestors) were trying mock a symbolizing protest in front of Bank of America. The police escorted us (the protesters) all the way up to 47th street from Zuccotti Park. Once we mad that turn down on 47th street, after marching – people started to stand in the street on getting arrested, so we (the protestors) can shut the block down. And what we wanted to do was make sure that the banks got a clear message on the notion that the people are tired of the abuse of the banks.

Holding that large protest in time square took a lot of people willing to give up their individual freedoms; to get arrested for a cause. The protestors, are now occupying Time Square, and while we are there: the police, felt the need to remove the people from the space. That might have been the biggest mistake, the New York City police commissioner made. They sent in the police horses, in to disperse the crowd of people. I was three rows of people behind the mounting of the horses. And in front of me were women and I couldn't get in front of them to stand mount. So I stood behind in support, and to hold the base—just in case the police tried to overpower the women. Even though in the frontline, men were holding the gates, and five rows of people support. Like jam pack—rows, meaning it could have been three rows of more people, jam back to fight off the police.

While the people, mounted a fight with the police horses—one of the police sergeants, said: if we (the people protestors) didn't move; they (the police) would send in the horses to disperse us. We (the people protestors) didn't move, and they (the police) sent in the horses. A fight broke out with the police, and their horses, with a man on the frontlines. And then one of the horses stomped a man as the police removed a barricade and tried to force the crowd to move. The crowd of we (the protestors) rush the police horses, and it was a shocking site to see—horses move backward and way from the people. I was like three rows of bodies (the protesters) away from this, so I had direct sight of the protest. When I saw that man underneath that horse getting stomped twice—I rushed to the front, but couldn't seem to get passed all of the women, rushing to the front as well.

And I guess when those horses saw a massive amount of people charging to the front of these barricades—those horses were frightened, and started to move backwards. And the horse that stomped the man ran in the other direction—plus was scared to move forward. The people have won, and the police called off the fight.

Although, the mission was to get in front of Bank of America—so we can set a stage for the protest. We (the protesters) were stopped from crossing the streets, and we (the protesters) fought off the police, to win the symbol of the day. After that something managed to merge, as people started to file off. The police brought in a massive crew of other officers in full blown riot gear—where they forcefully removed people from the protest. I had already left, and was on my way out of the area—when I heard loud screams. I tried to turn-a-round and rejoin the protest, but the police wasn't allowing anyone who left the area back into the area.

Yet, the when I got home, and checked out on the news I saw something with a former marine specialist: St. Thomas, yelling and screaming at the police. Saying, these are people, not soldiers of war, and if they wanted to fight a war, they should join the army. After looking at clips of that – I had to YouTube, the event where I saw, the after math of what happened on Times Square after I had left. This made me more vibrant, and more dedicated to marching and protesting against the abuses of Government. After looking what the police has or have done—the vow and fight came to be about up staging the police, in a non-violent protest.

Times Square battle was the first battle and marking for my journey with the New York City Police, and my first view of the strategy to denounce protesting. Or how NYC police and government officials will handle these types of protesting; in the streets in the biggest city of them all next to Tokyo Japan (New York City), these protest. I knew and saw how the police will handle the people, and monitored their strategies on enforcement. And it made me more aware of what the police would do, in order to break up and disperse the crowd or crowds of people. So in some of the sessions: behind the scenery I would email key officials in OWS or the New York General Assembly; and ask them to file in these key points. Those key points were to acknowledge how the police were going to attack the protesters, and take the strengths of the armed forces, away from them.

Yes, I wanted to make sure that the police didn't have the chance or right to arrest people for peacefully protesting. And I wanted to let the mayoral assembly know that the circus was in town. And the circus was nationally known, and internationally knows internet blogger—"TheFanNJ," was in town and the show has begun. I joined this movement to take over New York City, in a Martin Luther King Jr. style, of marching and creating havoc in New York City. And making this the staple center to how (we the protestors) was able to change the focus, plus dictate how the police interact with protestors.

And that day marked a day in history, where the people were able to make a shining mark. That day marked something that many didn't see coming, as we occupied the streets. Chanting—"Whose streets, Our Streets." Or the famous quote, "We are the 99%, You are the 99%," plus the "The people united will never be defeated, The people united will never be defeated." Or the quotes: "Banks got bailed out, the people got sold out."

The reason for this massive day of protesting was to symbolize the banks move to charge debt card fees on people's money marketing accounts, or personal banking accounts. Something that was never done before, and regularity not required by the banks, but since they were getting sited for cheating consumers—they felt the need to suck more money from the consumers, and people wasn't going to have that. And from that moment and time on the movement grew, and transformed into what we now know as Occupy Wall Street. And the movement transformed on that day, as it went from criminals, to outlaws and outcast –to an angry mob of people; on to hippies, and a bunch of people that didn't know what they want—into a mission to fight off corruption, while displaying their art; looking for social justice plus economic equality. The message was clear, students and middle-class America needed, and were looking for government to help their causes, and help manage their way of life—not favor the upper, super rich, or those that are impaired by the greed in capitalism.

Looking and monitoring the frontlines of this movement, making sure that my face didn't marginalize or take full credit for the movement – I needed to stay behind, but lead from inside. What many people will call, leading from behind, and that's what I wanted and needed to do? Since I have done something like this before, with the movement to lead Senator Barack Obama, on becoming the President of the United State! I thought it would benefit the movement if I gave my counsel, and gave my presence—not the structure, or the being, but support plus presence to The New York General Assembly while leading from behind. And by me fighting with them, marching in solidarity with them, will bring other elected leaders to the mix, and bring those who make the policies respect the occupants even more than before. My goal wasn't to be the leader or the president of Occupy Wall Street, but to make sure that their voices were heard, and respected by those who are not: occupying the streets.

Plus make sure that the perception and direction wasn't controlled by centralized media. People didn't want the perception and control of what was going on with Occupy Wall Street – to be portrayed as it was with News Corporation: better known as Fox News. Lots of people would say what does: Fox News have a play into this – well if you YouTube, Fox and Occupy Wall Street – you will get 13 reels or pages of commentary on the hatred, or mis-perception this news organization was displaying on the entire movement. The deck was stacked as soon as the protesters created their very first protest. When Fox covered the movement, it was about the perception of giving this a negative view. And making this a news story rather than a policy driven story, about economic insecurity, was one of the reasons why the perception was negative. So the fight with the perception of the movement went from the invasion of the police, and the lying misconceptions coming from media outlets. Even CNN news broadcasting center, had the mixed views of what Fox news been displaying.

If we understand the process of why people are protesting in the streets—then the general consensus will or should be about: how we got here in the first place. During the 101st Congress, the preponderant focus of the Finance Committee in the tax area was developing revenue-raising provisions to achieve significant, long-term deficit reduction as a part of the budget reconciliation process. The Committee also achieved the enactment of important tax policy reforms, including the repeal of the section 89 nondiscrimination rules, repeal and replacement of section 2036[c] estate freeze rules and enactment of a comprehensive package of energy production incentives. The Committee participated in other significant legislation initiatives of the Congress, including the Financial Institutions Reform Bill, the Clean Air Act Amendment, the Oil Pollution Act, the Puerto Rico Referendum Act and the Campaign Cost Reduction and Reform Act.

This allowed the same congress to draft a ruling for financial institutions – The Finance Committee was named to the conference on the Financial Institutions Reform, Recovery and Enforcement Act, (H.R. 1278). In the conference, the committee agreed to repeal the special tax rules (regarding FSLIC payments and tax-fee reorganizations) applicable to financially-troubled financial institutions as of May 10, 1989.

Again a lot of people wouldn't know what these small simple amendments to current amendments that are a part of a future installment to an actual bill. As what John McCain would call: Pork Amendments. Which are pieces of legislation that are crammed into an amendment, to hide the fact of a singular notion on a hidden agenda, represented by a sponsoring member of the House of Representatives? These are things get smoked into a package that may go unmonitored and become part of a public document, and if the president sign the legislation—that legislation will become public law. But as long as the amendment isn't signed by the president, it will remain a public document that immediately goes into effect.

Now you are wondering what does this have to do with Occupy Wall Street, or the movement. This have a lot to do with the general movement because it gave banks to much leverage, and place the people at the mercy of the banks. As said before, the banks or a financial firm can write off assets before the assets was sold, and then reap in the profits on fees, and charges in the aftermath. Like if you repackaged a loan, or anything dealing with financing a home, you were left at the mercy of unfavorable interest rates. And the banks were making in profits on 9% interest rates charged on bonds that they were getting from the treasury worth less than a dollar.

Which left people out in the cold because they were purchasing or repurchasing loans at a much higher rate— than ever before, way higher than the subprime crisis? This type of practice actually sent people that were below the water lines in terms of premiums on their mortgages, in social and economic collateral lost. Meaning they had no collateral, or credit to repackage or refinance their homes. What that actually means, is their homes were worth something, but their balance sheets, made them worth nothing – where they lost everything.

Which leaves us to the slogan spoken by those on these streets: "Banks got bailed out, while the people got sold out." How did the people get sold out, well a lot of people will take blame or make major focus on T.A.R.P. (troubled assets relief program), but that didn't start this problem of greed. It only gave it a door way, for manipulation and speculation. Banks or the top five banks brought each other out to manipulate the market. While they were manipulating the market, these banks weren't addressing the debt of the consumers on products they sold. So in terms, they speculated their market sheets to get a better profit on capital gains, then spent those capital profits on redevelopment credits at the state level. In other words, they were buying up your property, charging you outrageous fees, while taking out hidden and service fees in the process—where it made you lose money in the process.

People were looking at their nickels, and their dimes race out of their pockets by these banks; based on forever changing hidden contracts. Like the minimum balance for an account in Chase Bank was $5,000—they allowed people to open accounts for 7 months of free service. When that promotional period ended, without warning—Chase Bank would service fee you to death? And if you didn't use the account, you were charged for inactivity, and lets' say— you have been given fees which broughtout your financial death on where your account has a negative balance. If you don't make a deposit or show some type of activity within 10 days of the negative—they (Chase Bank) will close your account without even telling you, while they still charge you a hidden fee. And what I mean by the service fee charges were that you would make a deposit and a percentage of what you deposited—there was a fee attached to the transaction. So depending on how much you deposit into your account, there was a fee for that. It seems ridiculous to continue to make deposits into an account, while losing money on each deposit. (You are being charged for banking on every transaction)

Even though majority of that would come through some sort of speculation, or how the manipulation with the financial system allowed the market to get manipulated. Yet, what stop the insiders from government from doing the same type of trading. People were having more problems with the laws that monitor campaigns, and the power or money in these campaigns.

People always wondered why the movement to start occupants in the streets participated in events that went after the 1%. Occupy Wall Street (OWS) all the members participated in creating the conditions that brought us to this point. You see, that economy is a reflection of the connection between us. Therefore, trying to fix the economy without fixing the way we relate to each other is bound to fail.

Today, there's worldwide evidence in the form of economic collapse, political failure, and social unrest that humanity are going through a global change. As many experts are already seeing, the nature of that change is that we are becoming so interconnected and interdependent that the old egotistic systems that have brought us thus far are no longer working.

This is why the current economy, which promotes personal benefit above all, is no longer sustainable. "The pursuit of happiness is not a solitary goal. We are connected and so is our joy." –Prof. James H. Fowler, (Political and Social Scientist) Prof. James H. Fowler, is a supporter of the protesting students, and older citizens creating occupants that occupy the streets. And in order to continue to spread the message, the OWS crowd would gain support from prestigious members of the general electric when it comes to education. Since majority of their supporters where college students and it was hard for Professors, to say to their students, don't protest. Prof. Nicholas Christakis (Physician and Social Scientist) stated, "We were able to examine how in very fundamental ways, human beings can act like flocks of birds or stampeding buffalo." The meaning of this small gesture was to show that when it comes to money and finance—humans are like animals tripping over themselves, to mount the top.

Our interdependence has become a fact of life, But our way of thinking and our values, are still locked in the old paradigm. Therefore, the path to a viable solution must from aligning ourselves to embrace our mutual dependence and responsibility for other. Resisting it would have the same results as resisting gravity. Our interconnectedness nature is as much a part of our makeup as the network of neurons in our brains or hives of bees, in other words—if you're still not sure, try and see how many different countries have participated in the making of your clothes, your gadgets, your food, etc. Meaning in some way, we as people are dependent on the art, and labor of the other person.

Which makes our ways of life interconnected, or tri-dependent on the other in the social society of a global economy? Leaders of the Occupy protest had general ideas about: the numbers of researchers that have already shown the power of social influence. Now is the time to use this power in order to lift ourselves from the obsolete dog-eat-dog mindset, recognize the reality of an integrated human system, and adjust ourselves accordingly.

We must work together, using media, the internet and every means at our disposal to create a new environment that supports the new society we wish to establish. In the same way that our egotistic mindset has created everything around us, this new society will give birth to all the institutions and economic systems we will need. Only then, we can come up with the solutions that will bring about prosperity in the new world of interdependence. Paul Krugman, (Nobel Prize Laureate) in Economics; "We are all in the same boat." And judging from how this movement has grown during social media, and throughout the universities of the country—plus gain support throughout the country. Where they believed that the people who occupy the 1% didn't act on this social change in the economic fall alone? And they are right; the 1% had a lot of help. It's called greed and uncertainly – when those that trade in the exchange become uncertain of their investments, those same people tend to become a little greedier when trading their profits. And then reporting that loss or net gain on their capital gains returns.

These are the type of marginal rates that the people who occupy the streets called: Occupy Wall Street, have been protesting about. And as I listen to their cries and concerns, the movement to hold government accountable for the people that have abused corporate greed, and turned it into corporate mockery on economics. The economic structure for what people view as a corporation is at its best broken. And when you have a percentage of the country that have a distrust in the economics of the financial world, or have lost complete trust.

Documentary Script Scene:

After having that big debut and battle in Times Square New York on the National Day of Action in November, this trip in December was to make a statement to the President of the United States. President Barack Obama in December came to New York to have three big huge fundraisers. And he was at the Sheraton Hotel, on 57th street in New York. So our march through Time Square for the second time, made valued noise. People were trying to send a direct message to President Barack Obama about the money in politics. And how $30,000 plates as a campaign fundraiser was too much, and when the organizers of Occupy Wall Street got notice of who was on the list: Governor Andrew Cuomo, and Mayor Mike Bloomberg. This made me wanted to join the protest to create a down pore of rain on the Financial System.

While we were gathering at Bryant Park, one of organizers of the OWS movement, and leader of this event— what I saw was almost 2 thousand people showing up to rally against Mayor Bloomberg. When Mayor Bloomberg, went on public radio to state that the Occupy Movement is dying down, and when Former Mayor Rudy Gulliani stated that he would crush the Occupy Movement. It made more people more inspired to raise up and participate in the march. Yet the most shocking thing that made no headlines, was the illegal detainment set by the New York City Police Department. Myself, and many of the Occupy Protesters where caged in a corner and held at our own mercy for three hours. From 7pm, until 10:30pm, people were making random temper tantrum threats, and held against their will. They mocked the Police, and mocked Mayor Mike Bloomberg, and anyone else that didn't let them leave the area. What struck me was the moving action that the Chief of Police used to run down on the protestors. One the closed off the block, once me (and many of the protestors) entered into the area. Mainly myself, since I felt that I was the target.

They didn't allow the rest of the crowded 2000 protestors, after I and the people before me entered the targeted area. And then the police department moved in huge garbage trucks to block the view, and ongoing traffic, whether public or commercial. This made me more wary about what was about to go down. And it made me skeptical about the roles and rules of government. Whether or not the government and leader I gave my services too—actually respected me as a person, and the protesters behind me.

At that moment one of the protesters behind me saw a few of the New York City police mounting a station on the tier level of the restaurant underneath the hotel—which people may call the mezzanine area—with his riffle gun open, and nobody knew who the target was—but one of the protestors pointed it out. He said: "Look, there is an officer on that roof, and his pointing his gun." And that is when I knew, Omar Dyer was to become the imprinted leader of this movement. Imprinted as in terms of what Mayor Mike Bloomberg considers to be a threat. I was already on the list of hated activist by New Jersey's top mayors, as the public advocate that would need to be avoided.

End Script:

After that whole episode with the police and how they are treating the people, and remember this was before the incident that happened with Ex-marine Olsen. The Olsen story is a story that I will touch upon, because of the police abuse to him—resulted in people having this skeptical view of NYC police. The New York City Police Department has been know as being the toughest and bad boys on the block—where nobody or person can or would mess with them. Well, Omar Dyer a consensus and ever growing Nobel Scholar Electorate—brought a crushing blow to the NYC police department.

In another note during this march and movement for the Occupy nation was the protest in Oakland California. This story shocked the nation because he was a U.S. Marine (he as in Scott Olsen).

On October 25, 2011, Scott Olsen, a 24-year-old former Marine and Iraq War veteran, and a member of Veterans for Peace; suffered a skull fracture caused by a projectile that witnesses believed was a tear gas or smoke canister fired by the police of Oakland California. A video by protesters shows the explosion of what appears to be a flash-bang device thrown by one officer near protesters attempting to aid Olsen. The Associated Press later reported that it was not known exactly what kind of object had struck Olsen or who had thrown or fired it, but some protesters were throwing rocks and bottles. The Guardian reported that a projectile found near where Olsen fell was a so-called "bean bag round".

Olsen was rushed to the hospital by other protesters, who were fired upon with unknown police projectiles while attempting to aid him. Doctors at the hospital upon his arrival said that he was in critical condition. At least two other protesters were injured. The American Civil Liberties Union and National Lawyers Guild are calling for an investigation into the use of excessive force by Oakland police department. However, the investigation by the Citizens Police Review Board is expected to last several months. Details regarding Olsen's time in the U.S. Marine Corps are emerging. He served two tours of duty as a data network specialist in the Iraq War, was awarded seven medals (including the Navy-Marine Corps Achievement Medal), and received an administrative discharge as a lance corporal in November 2009 after serving four years.

Online records show that, while still on active-duty as a service member, Olsen became disillusioned with the Marines and created a now-defunct web site called; "I hate the Marine Corps."

Asked whether the web site resulted in his being administratively separated instead of receiving an honorable discharge, Olsen later told "USA Today," he would not comment because he is trying to get the discharge upgraded. About 2,000 people held a candlelight vigil for Scott Olsen in front of Oakland City Hall's administration building on October 27, 2011. Olsen was then released from the hospital around November 10, and is gradually recovering from his injuries but has difficulty speaking. On November 14, he posted a statement on a social networking site stating, "After my freedom of speech was quite literally taken from me, my speech is coming back but I've got a lot of work to do with rehab."

A video interview with Olsen, the first since his injury, was published November 28, 2011, on the San Francisco Bay Area Independent Media Center web site. In short order, Olsen was subsequently interviewed on three nationally televised cable news shows: MSNBC's The Ed Show (Nov. 29), MSNBC's The Rachel Maddow Show (TV series) (Dec. 1) and Current TV's Countdown with Keith Olbermann (Dec. 2).

This made lots of people write letters to the labor unions, and other organizations to come in support. I happen to run a political action committee—whereas, I also wrote a letter to the NAPO: National Association of Police Organization. They are in charge of the police conduct around the nation, and they are responsible for the public perception of how the people interact with the men hired to protect.   The letter gave great detail about the current problems that are happening with this occupy protest.

NAPO
National Association of Police Organization
317 South Patrick Street
Alexandria, VA 22314-3501
703-549-0775
Fax: 703-684-0515

From
Coaches! 101 (PAC)
PO Box 4463
Jersey City NJ 07304

As the officers acting on behalf of the mayors of these cities are now in violation of public law: (43 U.S.C. 1181(a); 30 U.S.C. 601 et seq.; 43 U.S.C. 1701): which states: *Upon timely filing of a protest, the authorized officer shall reconsider the decision to be implemented in light of the statement of reasons for the protest and other pertinent information available to him/her. The authorized officer shall, at the conclusion of his/her review, serve his/her decision in writing on the protesting party.* In New York City, Mayor Mike Bloomberg, leashed water, and horses on citizens in a civil protest – even after the protesters met the demands of the residents, and the officials.

Many of them were forced into search and seizure practices, without their rights being read to them: their Miranda Rights haven't been read to them, and a charge hasn't been given on them. Mayor Bloomberg has engaged in a public display of statements that violate our organizations right to protect the civil liberties of our representatives. The mayor of New York City violated: Pub. L. 107-174, (No fear Act) by engaging in political discourse on citizens without proper proof, stating such is a sanitation problem, or enforcing public boards to present or pass resolutions against civil disputes. Even when concessions were made! In Oakland California – protesters where flurried with tear-gas, and abuse of forces, as if they were at war with citizens protesting.

Many of those that are citizens are strapped because of the economic situation. A percentage of them are protesting their rights because they have problems with their mortgages, and the system that use to protect them, have now turned against them. You have students out there without jobs, and are looking for some help. They are not criminals or outlaws, and shouldn't be treated as such. This organization is demanding that the NAPO denounce the practices of riot gear for protesting citizens—while reforming how they communicate with protesting citizens.

1. Like making a what (Occupy Wall Street ask [a mic check])
2. Request a civil break up without force
3. Schedule a public meeting to hear their concerns
4. Treat them as humans, and not out-laws.

As a national organization that has fought hard for union labor, police salaries – and public jobs, we are sending you this letter for the first time, in order to prevent violent outbreaks with police and members of the Occupations across the nations.

This organization isn't the full right spokes organization of Occupy Wall Street: or Occupy Together, or the Police Officers of America: we are an advocacy group representing the safety of residents.

And they way officers are handling citizens is a safety concern, that needs change. And Omar Dyer has joined this protest in solidarity of their voice – our program protests the voices of those that go unheard.

After that incident with Scott Olsen, the movement gained more influence from unions and labor organizations. These organizations used the movement to spur dramatic change in the talks and legislation parts of what was happening with Wall Street Protests. People were inspired by this beating of a citizens, and who was once a U.S. Marine—even though that solider has gone rouge about his feelings on the service, but not his feelings about the country. The marches and rallies got a little bigger—plus it seemed like there was more support coming to the movement. And it looked like more super celebs were more interested in donation, participating—whereas the perception of the movement was dramatically changing. Changing in such a way that people were starting to respect the movement in general. And the perception has come or was coming down about the movement being a movement of radicals, and outlaws.

And they were getting more media coverage from all networks, outside of CNN Network, and Fox News. The reason why CNN backed off the movement because of the element of Social Media, more and more independent film-makers, and reporters starting joining the movement because of the notion that they wanted to follow one of the biggest bloggers in the world, and a current Nobel Scholar Electorate. I never knew that I would be able to generate a large following off of what I write on the internet. And joining the movement to occupy these streets—made me think about the great leaders of the past. Or now if I can be that leader that many have seen in my spirit—since I posses that spirit to lead, and I also posses that passion; with a great understanding to lead people!

The only problem is the notion that I am not in the same financial backings as those who have benefited from their leadership roles. I have the potential to raise a large sum of money, and the backing to do it—yet, my current situation; I couldn't raise ten bucks.

On October 15, tens of thousands of demonstrators staged rallies in 900 cities around the world, including Auckland, Sydney, Hong Kong, Taipei, Tokyo, São Paulo, Paris, Madrid, Berlin, Hamburg, Leipzig, and many other cities. In Frankfurt, 5,000 people protested at the European Central Bank and in Zurich, Switzerland's financial hub, protesters carried banners reading "We won't bail you out yet again" and "We are the 99 percent." Protests were largely peaceful, however a protest in Rome that drew thousands turned violent when "a few thousand thugs from all over Italy, and possibly from all over Europe" caused extensive damage. Thousands of Occupy Wall Street protesters gathered in Times Square in New York City and rallied for several hours. Several hundred protesters were arrested across the U.S., mostly for refusing to obey police orders to leave public areas. In Chicago there were 175 arrests, about 100 arrests in Arizona (53 in Tucson, 46 in Phoenix), and more than 70 in New York City, including at least 40 in Times Square. Multiple arrests were reported in Chicago, and about 150 people camped out by city hall in Minneapolis.

In the early morning hours of October 25, police cleared and closed an Occupy Oakland encampment at Frank Ogawa Plaza in Oakland, California. The raid on the encampment was described as "violent and chaotic at times," and resulted in over 102 arrests and several injuries to protesters. The city of Oakland contracted the use of over 12 other regional police departments to aid in the clearing of the encampment.

An Iraqi war veteran, Scott Olsen, was allegedly hit in the head with a teargas canister and suffered a skull fracture. His condition was later upgraded from critical to fair. The next night, approximately 1,000 protesters reconvened in the plaza and held marches late into the night. On November 2, protesters in Oakland, California shut down the Port of Oakland, the fifth busiest port in the nation. Police estimated that about 3,000 demonstrators were gathered at the port and 4,500 had marched across the city; a spokesman for the protest movement, who gave only his first name, told the BBC that he had heard people say that there were as many as 20,000 or 30,000 demonstrators, but added, "It's impossible to tell."

Then many people would like to know and see who the leaders of this movement are, and the names that follow behind Scott Olsen, are theses organizers. But one part of the movement that the general media left out, and what really help this movement was: Omar Dyer's personal organization. Coaches! 101 A NJ Non-Profit, was a major part in helping the vibe or changing the perception of the Occupy Movement. Even though many people had mixed opinions about the statehood of this corporation—and what it was about. Occupy Wall Street is about the growth of the people, and not the flow of money in statehood. Yet, what they didn't understand was the political capital that was being used for that right to liberty. And some of them were having that ban titles shoved in their face, and they didn't even know on some issues this group was fighting against its own protection.

As congress was more about killing, abandoning—or banning my small organization Coaches! 101 A NJ Non-Profit, and Coaches! 101 (PAC). I run a company called: Coaches! 101—which has been under attack by the Internal Revenue Service, and Congress in general. Plus the local leaders at the state level, and many of the misinformed people! They would make up wild accusations about the organizational rights that Coaches! 101 might have, and the notion that this isn't a corporate-statehood, but a personal livelihood.

Occupy Wall Street then made their move to place pressure on Congress, to make sure that there's no corporate statehood. And they then leashed an all out war on corporations, and how people incorporate themselves or their art. Yet, what made me blindly fight against or didn't follow the OWS movement is when they attack civilization. I am for the rights of the people but not at the expense of the collapse of a civilized society—especially when there's no alternative solution. Some of the leaders in this movement to occupy the streets such as: Occupy Wall Street—are these members; Justin Wedes, David Graeber, Philosopher King: "Though he was involved with the Occupy Wall Street movement from the beginning, 50-year-old Yale University anthropologist. Still, Graeber "has been one of the group's most articulate voices, able to frame the movement's welter of hopes and grievances within a deeper critique of the historical moment," *Bloomberg* writes of him.

While Graeber is still at Yale, the university didn't renew his contract for the 2012-13 academic year. In a Sept. 10 interview with Charlie Rose, Graeber said Yale never gave him an explanation for why they were not renewing his contract, though he said his students believe it was because of his support for a graduate student who wanted to start a union. These are some of the ideas that spur into the scenes, when people wanted to know who the leaders of this movement were.

Chapter 4:

Vulture Capitalism

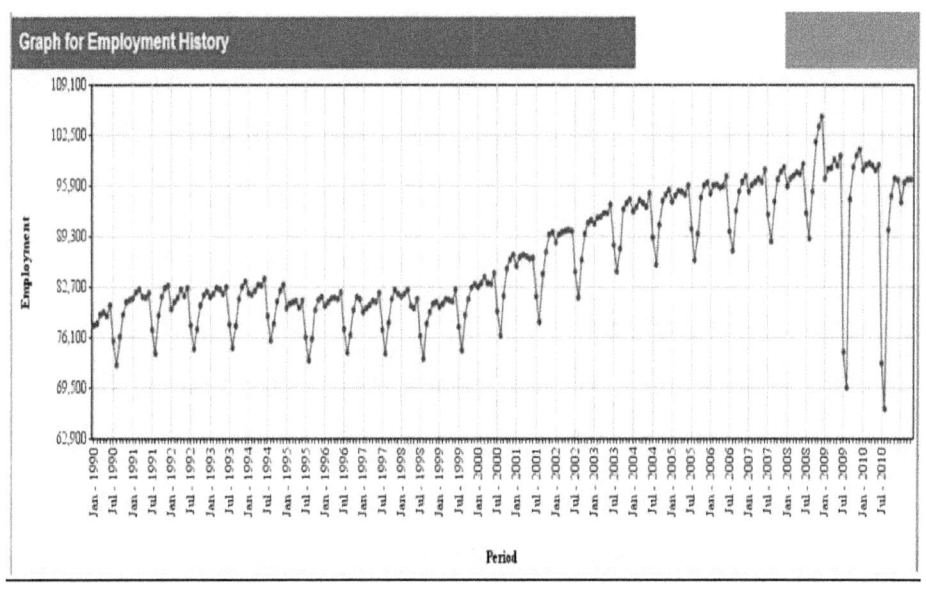

While people fight off the basis of what Wall Street Protester are doing, they are clouded by the underlining facts. Bank of America, used Merrill Lynch to get into these risky practices. Practices that took people's information, traded off to the highest marketer, and written off the transactions to make a profit! BAC, (Bank of America Corporation) -- On April 13, 2011, the Board of Governors of the Federal Reserve System (**"Federal Reserve"**) issued a cease and desist consent order (**"Consent Order"**) against Bank of America Corporation (**"BAC"**). The Consent Order makes no finding on any issues of fact or law or any explicit allegation concerning BAC. The Consent Order describes a consent order that the Office of the Comptroller of the Currency (**"OCC"**) and Bank of America, N.A. (**"BANA"**), which is owned and controlled by BAC, entered into addressing areas of weakness identified by the OCC in mortgage loan servicing, loss mitigation, foreclosure activities, and related functions by BANA. The Consent Order also states that the OCC's findings raised concerns that BAC did not adequately assess the potential risks associated with such activities of BANA. The Consent Order directs the board of directors of BAC to take appropriate steps to ensure that BANA complies with the OCC consent order.

The Consent Order requires BAC and its institution-affiliated parties to cease and desist and take specified affirmative action, including that BAC or its board: (1) take steps to ensure BANA complies with the OCC order; (2) submit written plans to strengthen the board's oversight of risk management, internal audit, and compliance programs concerning certain mortgage loan servicing, loss mitigation, and foreclosure activities conducted through BANA; and (3) periodically submit written progress reports detailing the form and manner of all actions taken to secure compliance with the Consent Order. BAC submitted an offer of settlement to the Federal Reserve.

In the offer of settlement, BAC agreed to consent to the entry of the Consent Order, without the Consent Order constituting an admission by BAC or any of its subsidiaries of any allegation made or implied by the Federal Reserve in connection with the matter.

BANA Foreclosure Practice Order

On April 13, 2011, the OCC issued a cease and desist consent order ("**Order**") against BANA. The Order identified certain deficiencies and unsafe or unsound practices in residential mortgage servicing and in BANA's initiation and handling of foreclosure proceedings. The Order finds that in connection with certain foreclosures of loans in it is residential servicing portfolio, BANA; (a) filed or caused to be filed in courts executed affidavits making various assertions that were not based on the affiants' personal knowledge or review of relevant books and records; (b) filed or caused to be filed in courts numerous affidavits or other mortgage-related documents that were not properly notarized; (c) litigated foreclosure proceedings and initiated non-judicial foreclosure proceedings without always ensuring that the promissory note or the mortgage document was properly endorsed or assigned and, if necessary, in the possession of the appropriate party at the appropriate time; (d) failed to devote sufficient resources to ensure proper administration of its foreclosure processes; (e) failed to devote to its foreclosure processes adequate oversight, internal controls, policies and procedures, compliance risk management, internal audit, third party management and training; and (f) failed to sufficiently oversee third-party providers handing foreclosure-related services.

The Order requires that BANA cease and desist such practices and requires BANA's Board to maintain a Compliance Committee that is responsible for monitoring and coordinating BANA's compliance with the Order.

The Order provides for BANA to: (a) submit a comprehensive action plan that includes a compliance program, third-party management policies and procedures, controls and oversight of BANA's activities with respect to the Mortgage Electronic Registration System and compliance with MERSCORP's membership rules, terms, and conditions; (b) retain an independent consultant to conduct an independent review of residential foreclosure actions regarding individual borrowers; (c) plan for operation of management information systems; (d) submit a plan for effective coordination of communications with borrowers related to loss mitigation or loan modification and foreclosure activities; (e) conduct an assessment of BANA's risks in mortgage servicing operations; and (f) submit periodic written progress reports detailing the form and manner of all actions taken to secure compliance with the Order. BANA submitted an offer of settlement to the OCC. In the offer of settlement, BANA agreed to consent to the entry of the Order, without admitting or denying any wrongdoing.

*Gail Cahaly, et al. v. Merrill Lynch, Pierce, Fenner & Smith Incorporated ("**Merrill Lynch**"), Benistar Property Exchange Trust Co., Inc.("**Benistar**"), et al. (Massachusetts Superior Court, Suffolk County, MA)*

Plaintiffs alleged that Merrill Lynch aided and abetted a fraud, violation of a consumer protection law, and breach of fiduciary duty allegedly perpetrated by Benistar, a former Merrill Lynch client, in connection with trading in the client's account. During the proceedings, plaintiff also made allegations that Merrill Lynch engaged in sanctionable conduct in connection with the discovery process and the trial. In 2002, following a trial, a jury rendered a verdict for plaintiffs. Thereafter, the Court granted Merrill Lynch's motion to vacate and plaintiffs' motion for a new trial.

On June 25, 2009, following a retrial, the jury found in plaintiffs' favor. On January 11, 2011, the Court entered rulings denying plaintiffs' motion for sanctions and punitive damages, awarding certain plaintiffs consequential damages, and awarding attorneys' fees and costs. On February 7, 2011, the Court issued final judgment requiring Merrill Lynch to pay $9,669,443.58 in consequential and compensatory damage plus statutory interest, and $8,700,000 in attorneys' fees and costs; but denying plaintiffs' requests for punitive damages and sanctions.

The client, a co-defendant, filed a notice of appeal of the Court's denial of its motion for a new trial on or about January 19, 2011. On or about January 24, 2011, plaintiffs filed a notice of appeal of the Court's denial of their motion for sanctions pursuant to Mass. Gen. Laws c. 231 § 6G. On March 1, 2011, the plaintiffs filed a notice of appeal of the Court's denial of their requests for punitive damages and sanctions, and the Applicant filed a notice of cross-appeal on March 15, 2011.

What a lot of people didn't know, or are clueless on where the notions in writing that expel some of these theories. That consumers have had their rights violated at the expense of capitalism. The sub-prime loan crisis, not only went into a market it shouldn't have—but the debts were written off on creditors accounts, sent to collection agencies—where all parties made a profit.

Understanding the truth:

The truth of the matter is you as a consumer went to Bank of America, and purchased a home equity loan, personal loan (money marketing account) or credit from the bank. The bank wrote off your expenditures, sent that note to a private lender (Merrill Lynch) and got a tax bond to pay you.

Merrill Lynch wrote off your assets, or placed them in pool of likely loans. What are likely loans, they are loans with high premiums called: (Sub-prime) and these sub-prime loans have long and lengthy payment options (more than 10 years) and they are placed in a public auction—which is also known as sent to a collection agency. Merrill Lynch would get a profit sharing Surety Bond for loaning you the consumer. Surety Bonds are 100% repayment bonds for loans under $10,000. Also, known as municipal bonds, and after they have been sold off to a different agency, and off the balance sheets of the holders of the notes: BAC and Merrill Lynch, your information was sent to an offshore agency or an account, and sold. That would mean, a future payment for the bond holder, and a quick fix payment for the note exchange.

This practice is widely disregarded, and only used by large banks: Merrill Lynch, Bank of America, Goldman Sachs, Chase Bank, Wells Fargo, and banks under the jurisdiction of Morgan Stanley. People who naturally don't understand the process, will know that five corporations, control your debt, and reap in profits outside of the normal day of banking. This is a side deal, and a transaction that has nothing to do with the process and orders of the banking industry. It's a way that they can create easy cash growth, in order to buy state tax credits, and make an appearance of profit gains, in order to get share holders to invest more funds into their company.

In short terms, a bank would use the notes they write off—to increase profit sharing, where they then brought state tax credits that allowed them to increase employment or increase executive compensation. Yet, the problem was the trading of your debt to a public auction (collection agency) is now an illegal practice. When you deal with a fully functional bank – they are not allowed to send your debt to a collection agency: (Public Auction). Because at a public auction millions of notes are packaged together known as derivatives, and sold in bulk at a discount price.

And that would leave you at a disadvantage, because you have no control of the payback options, and are subjected to harassing calls, plus contracts that have been written by the same agency. Now lots of people have been walked into a loan package that they didn't understand, had no resources to pay them off—plus became victims of a scheme by two financial firms, looking to make a short term buck, at the expense of a public trade. Debt that use to be private, and with entities and one person, is now public debt. Public debt is money that is owed to the public, and this is one of the major reasons—why our debt crisis is high. Because of the fact that private corporations, packaged people's debt into a public note without a long term payment plan (Merrill Lynch). Thus making an appearance that the bank made a profit, when they only sold off the responsibly of your debt.

This is the type of capitalism that made the members staging in protest, to actually come-out and protest on. They are not made at the system, they are disrupted by the corruption in the system—where greed gets rewarded, while hard workers are seeing their nickels and dimes walk out of the pockets. And this is what the entire occupy movement was against. People in the movement weren't against the growth of capitalism, or how big large corporations managed to create or accumulate their wealth. They were more concerned in the way and approve that bankers are managing to raise profit margins, while not giving the consumer any product. Which is more than likely a back door trading deal? When I join this movement I was more inspired by the amount of people that engaged in this movement. People were so inspired to do something about the wealth and the distribution that went down. Plus the civil liberties that where being harmed in the process. I wasn't expecting to see a monumental growth of elders, student, poor—homeless and concerned citizens, rally behind an idea. I wasn't expecting to see celebrities of all kinds rally behind a voice.

Occupy Wall Street: Growth of Leader: Wall Street Occupied

Some people may say that leaders are grown from their actions. And during this movement and looking at all of these people follow—12 leaders, who in directly acted in coordination with each other. Which made this movement very special because of the fact that there wasn't a true leader subscripted to the focus point of the movement? You had a lot of trade unions in the movement doing everything that they can do in order to help the movement grow. You had the teachers unions working hard to make sure that they movement didn't lose its muster. And what was shocking to see that many of the other leaders in the world couldn't predict was a growth and companionship from the leaders in the religious group.

The Jewish parishioners were contempt to hide their differences with their counter parts in Palestine –for the common good. You had those that where Jewish, and many that were Islamic in one park protesting a giant entity. (Wall Street Bankers)... You had evangelicalism, morons, Baptist, Penicoastal, atheists, Catholics, and Christians all in one park protesting for economic equality. Since the social injustice in this country and around the world has gone in a stray to favor the interest of those who bank in the industry. An industry that was built to create a perception of wealth distribution! A distribution that created super rich, and desperately poor. A group of middle class citizens that were falling by the waste-line, and slowly disappearing. They are watching their income stay stagnant – while they see everything from a bar of soap rise in cost.

The thing that made this movement grow was that the diversity of the groups and the people logged in this movement. People that came from all walks of life—you even had Buddhist monks in the movement spreading the word of God. In New York City's Zuccotti Park, something really special happened that should be remembered for all times.

What went down in the park was more about the fight against greed. But it was one of the greatest sights to see, and one of a magical moment to be a part of—was happening in the park. You couldn't go anywhere in the world and get that many people, from different cultures, beliefs to fight for one common cause. You can't get that many different ideologies and perceptions to talk and counter act with each other without a confrontation—yet, in this park people who had different beliefs and different views, came together to talk about the social economic inequality that was happening in the world.

The main reason why many people were engaging in the massive protest that happens in Zuccotti Park is because of the people. Occupy Wall Street really inspired a world to protest, and during that inspiration lots of people came together in unity. Blacks, Whites, Asians, elders, younglings, and anyone who have been harmed by the greed and corruption happening on Wall Street, flocked to Zuccotti Park. This became a symbol for people who were losing their homes, and needed to spread; share or have a message, better yet need a place to vent frustrations on what the system is doing to them. How they were turned away and their lives were being turned upside down. And this movement plus message made a symbol of the depression the middle class was facing at the hands of those who made profit on Wall Street.

My very own journey leads me to sympathize with many of the protesters, and become either a part of their cause or with their respective cause.

All movements have a point, and they have a special place. What made the Occupy Movement more impactful was the leadership of women? Women have been a crying call on respect, equal wishes, plus interactive solutions. Yet, the struggle of female equality shouldn't be about bashing and pushing—plus labeling allies.

Amy Goodman

One of the most vocal voices in the Occupy Movement was Amy Goodman. She was like the Virginia Wolf of this movement. She put the chips in place, spread the voices—made the calling cries, rallied other women, plus became the star voice. She is Occupy Wall Street, and there were many other females taking part in the organization parts of this fantastic movement. Because in order for the many to flock in a common space—women had to organize the roles of leadership. Amy Goodman often spoke on cable channel called: Democracy Now! Which is an independent news organization that gives open news reporting not covered in the mass media audiences—she covers in great deal what the movement is about?

Her voice is heard among her peers that range in the thousands. Her image is viewed as the best in the movement in general, as to know—if you're not a part of or have been in the OWS movement; you wouldn't know who she is; or what she was about? Before I started viewing and monitoring the movement, I had no clue who she was—or what her ideology was generally about. Most importantly, I didn't even know her voice and show was that widely popular in the journalist business. I am a film-maker not a political journalist. I'm an activist by trade and birth, but politics wasn't my craft until I was placed on the national stage in 2009. So knowing who these political pundits were became a fetch for me, and while at one of the protest—someone started talking about her. And I felt ashamed that I didn't know who she was –so after that moment I began to immediately investigate who she was and what she was about.

Yet, she wasn't the singular or most important female in the movement. There were others, and it became increasingly hard to discover who these females are—or even interact with them. Many of them are unemployed, underemployed—stay at home moms, or over educated artist without an industry.

A lot of them are single, separately single—divorced, or transgender—plus many of them were feminist. They come from all religious backgrounds; many of them are from Islamic faith, while a lot of them Christians, and Atheist. A lot of them where free spirits, while a majority of them were reverse sexist, on how the perceived men, or how men treat them. Sometimes forcing men that believe in helping to walk away, and feel guilty for helping at all.

I believe a strong woman should be tough, strong and mindful—yet, the strip of power shouldn't undermine and label those who would want to be your allies. And Occupy Wall Street has been one of those movements that allowed the progression of when in these streets. It became an idea, as they would say: "Whose time has yet to come?" The movement in many parts scared me, because of the elements of separatism, vultures on anarchism, and those who were against government establishment. In reality, the movement is moved by women—Occupy Wall Street does have a lot of women in the movement. And there have been a lot of problems protecting them in this movement against sexual, physical, and emotional abuse. There have been a lot of cases of Rape, and adultery by women who didn't want to participate in sexual confrontations, and women who were dominatrix and participating in sexual confrontations. I believe in the singular notion that the future of this country and the leadership on how we interact will be dominated by the element of organization and women. One day maybe not today, or even in this decade, but we see a female rise above the pack and lead.

And I would be right behind that candidate, that leader and shaping her for the bruising battles that men will leash on her. And that's what inspired me about Occupy Wall Street. It was the fact that women, out - numbered the men, and forced many of the men—to fight on the frontlines.

My goals and focus was to make sure that the perception of Wall Street was a positive one. Since they made general conclusion and expositions that the movement was captured and cultured by culprits and anarchist. Like people who wanted to ran free and run a muck—or mock the global society. And that's not the real perception of what the term: "We are the 99%," came from. And even Times Magazine structured a statement on an idea in Egypt, as a man burnt himself because of the oppression coming from his presidential leader. A leader that was a friend to the United States, and what nobody expected was an idea of support to turn into a monumental cry about health and poverty. And if you took a look at the problems faced by those who occupy cities—they have bad health care, and progressive poverty, with unemployment issues.

Although, in my journey plus tour with Occupy Wall Street – I managed to listen to the people, and drafted a song called "Freedom Ring," which was drafted on a song sung in Egypt! Which was about, We the people, are free—down with capitalism, free the people? I wasn't in the notion of banning capitalism—yet I was more on the practicality that social economics and socio-economic played a large part in wealth distribution. That the theory of working hard, achieving the greater dream, and providing for your family was being turned upside down by the greed of the super rich; and I am not one that is about favoring hatred to the super rich. I am about caring and helping those that are having a hard time and making sure that nobody is left behind and that is why I become so interested in Occupy Wall Street. Because we are starting the vibe and notion to leave our women, children—plus the poor in the door that is left behind.

And hanging out with a lot of the protesters, you would and could sense that natural feeling that many were getting left behind. A lot of them were young and just starting out—getting into the process, and looking for an place to go.

A lot where young girls, who had no other alternative—plus the job market really didn't favor them on their future aspirations! And the craft of what they wanted to achieve, wasn't a reliable means of income. Since some women, or occupants, never dreamed of becoming an investment banker; in order to make a living. And a lot of them surely didn't want to enter into a health care field in order to make or keep payments on their student loans. While majority of them are in the entertainment business, who don't have a traditional shot at getting quality care coverage?

They came-out and bared it all, shown their postures, and goodwill shapes, in name of a movement. Men were actually flocking to camps because women were baring it all for the general idea of OWS, and the movement. By the end of the year, when the movement started in September, people have been searching for the person of the year. Times Magazine gave a different perspective on who the person of the year should be and they called that person: "The Protester." While they were looking for the single person in charge of these massive protests, or the leader joining and rallying the people, the editor couldn't find the one protester in New York City to single out as that protester? So they took a picture of a woman, who wore a scarf on her face. This was after that woman, came back from a protest that shut down Wall Street-for 15 minutes.

They then altered the picture to look like this: see figure below:

Occupy Wall Street: Women in OWS: Wall Street Occupied

The movement ended the year on a high note—that this was a serious vibe and a serious force in the future. As people started to realize that maybe the people protesting had a point, and maybe we as a nation should start listening to the disparities in how we accumulate wealth. And many of those who are women in this movement are young in age, they are inspired by the notion that we as the people – can rise above the electric. And we the people can flow to a new theory of how we treat the poor, respect our women, and be a part of that notion of transparency in government. As women played a large and vital role in these actions—whom had health problems from nursing our children! And were often stricken to live in poor or poorest situation based on their conditions of economics, and the domains life has given them.

These are the people in the frontlines, who fight hard – march harder, and believe in economic equality; as they flock to these events in New York City. And majority of them are members of the elite that fight against the police. I'm mean, they are really heading the front lines, and they are in front of the men—doing most of the yelling and screaming. The movement sparked lots of interest when these women, made the men of Occupy Wall Street feel ashamed. That's when the movement became interesting— yet, the major focus was trying to keep the rhetoric, and flavor in a positive factor. And keeping the idea of busting up everything in order to make the news, out of the spectrum—plus not the major focus or perception of the movement was important to me. Since, in the real worked, lots of people where harmed by the practices of the larger financial institutions. This movement wasn't about me, the writers—or the women it's about and was always about social economic—plus economic equality.

Since the majority of this book is about my view and perception plus travels in Occupy Wall Street Movement. You need to learn and now who I am and what I stand for on critical issues. I am an activist, a revolutionist, and documenter—who has written memoirs on events or campaign stopping grounds. I was a former campaign adviser (volunteer) to Senator Barack Obama. Who also ran for Governor in the State of New Jersey in 2009—while failing to make the ballot! I then ran for state assembly, and set up my company's political action committee. And during the ground making of this committee, I took part in public advocacy. And become a corporate public advocate. And used Facebook, as a platform to stage my congressional bid, plus keep me in the status for the national state run for a nomination on the Gubernatorial Election.

My fight for the people has given me this natural title of the man of the people. And I wrote a song called: "The People," which was about the fight and mockery of the 99% from the leadership in New York City. Where it was slogans from the movement that said: "Bloomberg beware there's occupants everywhere, (We are the 99%) You are the 99%; All day all week occupy wall street. It became the national anthem of occupy Wall Street, and my hit song called: "Take Back Congress," on my ranging campaign—plus roles for the movement. I have always been an artist in the game of fame. Yet, my name has or was never mentioned in the system of working artist. I was never the best rapper when I got into the market. I wasn't the best singer, when I was in high school, or followed music. I wasn't the best dancer or could even dance as good as others, when I was asked for advice on dance groups. I am surely not the greatest speller in the world when it comes to proficient grammar. But one thing I will for every say is: I am the best writer and story teller since the early 10th century. And I had a gift to entertain people, which they would believe in my passion to lead. While I was a good story teller—I never wanted to take on the roles of leading.

Since no true leader is ever ready to lead a massive crowd of people. And nobody wants to follow someone based on words alone—since people would want to see action. While I wasn't the most talented person in my field, I did always had that sway, swag and look on me. I was definitely a ladies' man—with great skin. I would always tease the ladies, about how sexy I was, and that I had the looks of a Greek God. So I knew that I would and could find away to lead if I was ever given a chance. And people knew that once you gave me a leadership role in any place—it would be hard for me to give up those roles. Like, Michael Jackson—being given the microphone at the age of 5. For me in some ways I was given this role to unite and lead. When I was five years old, family members use to give me books to read. Like the auto-biography of Malcolm X. Shabazz. I couldn't understand the book, or even know the words I was reading—yet I had the ability to pronounce them. Imagine a 6 year old boy reading a book, that some college professors may have had trouble reading at that time. Again, I didn't know what I was reading, but I saw the words and was able to pronounce them.

At that age the world of books in an African American perspective—gave me that imaginary illusion that one day I would lead a generation to the Plymouth Rock in America's social justice system. When I read one of Martin Luther King Junior's books, and learned how he won the Nobel Peace Prize? I said to myself, and made a promise to myself, that one day—dead or alive; that prize will be mine. I have been grooming myself for the Nobel Prize since I was 6 years of age. And reading any book, I could get my hands on—which I was labeled the book worm, and generally teased by others as: Professor Dinker, Donker. Was I smarter than the average bear—more intelligent the rest? No I wasn't as smart as them or even on their level of intelligence—as the only thing I had going for me was my ability to pick things up on the fly.

I guess that gave me this apparent move and idea of what a true leaders are about. And I have done some research on my name: Omar (in Latin, Egyptian, Islamic, Roman Catholic, Buddhism, and Judaism) meant: King of Kings, Lomant, meant to lead among leaders, while Dyer was leader among Leaders.

Which basically meant, if you put me in a room with a bunch of leaders, where they all had egos, and gave a tally on which leader would come-out on top (Omar Dyer), would be that leader? I mean I had to deal with the leadership roles of my older brother—and he couldn't stop me or knock me back from being the leader of the family. Even when I was in a classroom, people would generally look to me to lead the classroom in chatter on learning. Since I would ask the right question, and then follow up the question until the consensus formed the correct answer. Even though I was born to lead, and had this dream and passion to win a Nobel Prize, or even win multiple Nobel Prizes. I always worked hard at what I ever I did, and never pounded my chess or tried to take full credit. I was just happy to have my name mentioned.

And when a group I participated in won that task and my name wasn't mentioned—I would get offended, and work harder to make sure that I would stand out amongst the crowd. I could latterly see myself, leading and becoming this great inspirational leader of all times. And I wanted that way back when I turned 10 years old, to have my name placed beside the greatest leaders ever. Like Martin Luther King Jr. or Gandhi, Alexander the Great, Jesus, Mosses, and many others in generations past. But my goal was to surpass them, and bring about a level of hope and happiness that they world has never seen. I wanted to be that leader of the next generation.

But that wouldn't craft people into believing that Omar Dyer, a small African American boy, in poverty – who was classified as psychotic child—who suffers from chronicle learning disorders, or even a child with attention disorders.

I mean some of the times—many of those that taught me would also classify me as a child with a learning disability, or a kid that suffers from Dyslexia. I wasn't stupid, I knew what Dyslexia meant—like not in the full description, but I knew—it meant I was slow and stupid. Since that word was often used in Martin Luther King Junior's book. Where the book talked about teachers telling Martin that he would be better served if he were a carpenter? But Martin had other plans—he wanted to teach, or that's what I learned from what was written.

Well I wanted to lead? I wasn't ready to lead, but I knew how, and I knew that working hard in getting people to believe in your leadership is a craft that many leaders today, still haven't figured it out. And me at the age of 12, I learned how to innovate and inspire people to follow my lead. I also, knew that with great leadership comes great responsibility, and I was ready for it. I remember going off to camp one year, and while at this camp—we had to form a bond of friendships. A group of boys wanted to sleep outside and camp out under the stars. Nobody wanted to do it because they were scared. Yet, I was the first one to grab my sleeping bag, and fall asleep in the middle of the camp.

And when I woke up the group of boys followed me. And the camp counselor told me, that I was brave – and that he has been trying to get people to sleep outside of the cabinets for years, and this was the first time he got a group to do it. Yet, that was just the beginning of my leadership qualities. And you're wondering what does this have to do with this Occupy Wall Street movement. Well, years before this movement came into the spotlight and spectrum—I went on a crusade telling anyone that would listen about how much of a bubble and trouble the housing markets was going and folding into. Again, the labels came—I was called crazy, and mocked, plus mimics made my views skeptical.

And the simple notion that my progress and battle only become more clear—when I had my encounters with Bank of America. Well, if you didn't know—I went to Bank of America to open an account with them in regards to a personal loan, which was used on an estate investment. Now Bank of America is not allowed to engage in that type of lending, without full disclosure. While my accounts went into inactive status—Bank of America, sent my account to a collection agency, then charged off the accounts on personal assets. But that didn't stop them from packaging those bad investments, and selling the notes in a bungle to A.I.G Insurances. Well we all knew what happened to A.I.G. securities were bailed out by the American currency exchange. What did A.I.G. do with the terms, they resold, assets to Merrill Lynch, then Merrill Lynch, swapped funds by buying out Bank of America? And what that left for you, these bankers made money off your debt, while you or me—suffered in courts and being harassed by collection agencies. And some of these collection agencies where limited liability companies—who brought your debt without notice in a bulk and used that information to invade your private bank accounts. Like, linking family members together, and going to the court system to garnish payment from your accounts. Now this wasn't legal until 1998, when the same members of the board that monitors credit—held positions in the court system, and lobbied for federal protection against using public boards, to garnish payments.

And when Bank of America, sold my debt to Pressler and Pressler, while the same agency used that information to buy up what was on my credit report. They then turned around, and used that same practice to buy up a family members debt—while then fusing and merging the members together, in order on getting into their private bank accounts. Well, in Hudson County, if you're political – you become a target for dirty politics.

But instead of arresting me, they arrested my elder brother. And Pressler sent me a notice that I will be arrested and had to pay a fine with the county sheriff's department in New Jersey. I went to the local court house to file a complaint, and spent the whole year investigating and digging up facts to prove my claims. And when I dug up the facts, more and more things started to come out about this dangerous practice that was brewing in the mix. This was a practice that has now been turned into an illegal method; of infringing on people's rights, plus their personal credit. I started to blog on this issue, and lots of people called me insane—while a lot of others, staged their one complaints. And it became very much clear, that a lot of them had no place to vent their frustration, or believed that nobody was listening to them. Until Now! There was a sense of attention coming to the fight and cause they were talking about, and judges where now willing to listen at the state levels on these type of laws and rules. And when I found out that Occupy Wall Street was fighting against those same principals—I knew, that this was the moment and time to energize an electric to take on the big banks.

Since in 2007, I had good credit, where the score was above 680, and just below 750 as a ficso score! Yet, that wasn't the major problem; banks were refusing to do business with me in a business method. I couldn't get a 7(a) business loan because of how Pressler and Pressler, manipulated my credit report, to being terrible, and worse that what the report actually looked like. And instead of improving the report—they were hell bent on making matters worse—because I challenged them in court. But what I found out is that many people were tricked, bamboozled into purchasing this risky loan packages, while bankers exchanged the notes—like candy in the Willy Wonka Chocolate factory. And, getting away with taking people out of their homes, because their mortgages where packaged with bad loans. And I then noticed that many of those who are losing their homes—are now strong and holding occupations in cities.

As we embark on a mission to bring the people's change into our democracy. We are forced to recognize and work with some of the basic principals—where some of these ideological ideas are the center points for social justice. And one of the major reason why I became committed to protest with OWS, was the fact that we brought the topic and equation of social equality back to the table, and at the for front of these conversations. Information from Occupy Wall Street—in what they called: Occupied Wall Street Journal: "The Growth of Capitalism," class, & Class struggle for (ex) dummies: written by libcom.org. At its root, capitalism is an economic system based on three things: wage labour (working for wages), private ownership of the means of production (things like factories, machinery, farms, and offices), and production for exchange and profit. Although I (Omar Dyer) don't necessarily believe that the growth of Capitalism is a root of all evil. Or is the root of disproportionate economic wealth.

Since Capitalism isn't the problem – its greed and corruption that leads to a problem. True capitalism leads to what many in this Occupy Wall Street movement, wanted. They wanted to groom and grow self production, or good capital principles to create jobs, and growth in a civilized manner. Like what confused me with this movement was the simple notion that they were biting the same hand that fought for them. And got confused on what a civilized setting and country meant, compared to what anarchist movement is about. The freedoms we see and have in this country, is far more than any civilized society around the world. We have a right to step away from terrene, and that simple right or gesture to protest in a civil manner, about our government. We have a system of public control over leaders in our government. Our system allows regular citizens to make a declaration—then make a public calling for action against the abusive government leadership in the court of law. Many systems or nation, do have a people driven democracy.

And that's what made me wanted to protest—it made me want to join the fight, and made me believe in a movement that brought the idea of social economic equality to a nation—walking in the winks and ways of a two society country. A country, were you having those who have, and many who have not. Since capitalism's appeared growth of wealth became this scrutinizing method—used to win elections, as the Republican Party has become an embarrassment of a party in the United States.

I am a logical historian, and know the basic principles of economic growth. And the grand-old republican party has turned south from the traditional roles. Why, because the leadership of the Republican Party has either been hijacked or confused about the ideal principles on economic wealth, and how the monetary exchanges works. And by them twisting and confusing facts, in order to make political points—in order to win an election, turned the country in a place of divided country of our leadership confusion; and how they treat the people. And that's why I am encouraging you the people, to break out those walking shoes, and march—protest (civil obedient protest), share your stories; while being a part of history in the making. And not watch the story from the sidelines.

And know that if you believe in the ideas, and principles on that notion of making an economic change in your life—you have the power to stand up and fight for it. As one of my favorite quotes say: "You can't vote for change on election-day: You have to get up and fight for it." Since the type of people's change don't come without passion, heart, and believing in something—even if you can't see nothing. And if you are having a troubled time in monitoring your economic situation—there are steps and keys or tools you as person can use to utilize you enormous efforts on stabilizing your financial health.

One thing about me, and writing books and memoirs—are what people like about my jargons. They love the fact that you will get a moralizing speech somewhere in the documentation. This speech called, "Will You Occupy for Justice," is about why we as the people made a choice to occupy.

Will You Occupy for Justice

As we the people came together and mocked a symbol of hope and passion for life, plus solidarity to the people. We came to New York City, and staged a protest. We the people protested against these mal-practices of the banking system. We fought against the corruption of greed in capitalism—plus the perception the rich had on the middle class. We as people believed in fighting for the middle class, and the struggling poor. Our fight, against the financial industrial system—isn't a fight against capitalism; or the overthrow on who is wealth plus the many that are poor. This fight should always be about economic security, and the power of the people to demand a fare and cleaner government. As I rehash an old statement:

The People are tired I say, (They are tired of what) -- They are tired of being brought by politics.

If you are tired of having your cultural beliefs, the right to worship any religion you choose, plus the moral right to your personal health. You as a person shouldn't be subjected to the political trials, and religious trial binaural on a public display—to what you do with your bodies. And religious prosecution should never be a political tool, to divide the people from worshiping their God.

The People are tired I say, (They are tired of what) -- They are tired of being brought by politics.

Tired of leaders favoring corporate interest, because of what has been donated to their re-election campaign fund. Tired of leaders, mocking the poor—while jazzercising the same corporate interest that lobbied their campaigns. Tired of special favors for those who incorporate the art of thievery—while mocking the lives of the poor and middle class. Tired of using investments as a tool to segregate the passion of the people. Tired of those who live in the 1% while you have others that occupy the world of the 99%. Tired of record profits from the banking system that bet against your financial health—in a system that gets paid whether you fail or gain success. Like Bank of America— reaping in $4.8 billion dollars in charging 10% in hidden fees on your money marketing accounts, debt accounts, and home equity accounts. While taking $64 billion dollars in T.A.R.P. funds, to bail out their board room debts, while forcing many people into equity problems, that led to homes being foreclosed on! If you are tired of a bank, reaping profits off of your financial misery—then you can understand why people are occupying the streets.

The people are tired I say, (They are tired of what) -- They are tired of being brought by politics.

People are tired of our candidates for president using these religious principles that impact matters on social liabilities, as a marketing tool—to hamper the faith our your elected president. Yes we believe in the ideas that government shouldn't be in the people's bedroom. While the faith and beliefs of the people, shouldn't be marketing tool on mocking someone's faith. The health of our daughters' and mothers' bodies should be a family matter between the house of worship and the family. Not a tool, to divide some people from others based on the church and where that religious entity stands in politics. And the house of worship should never be in presidential campaigns. And candidates should have moral obligations to respect the sanctity of our public policies and religious beliefs, when it comes to family

Public Policy should never be a tool to swift vote the people from their leaders. And it's against the principles set by the Catholic Church, to intrude people's lives with matters on family values—to incorporate them into political persuasion. Since a spiritual cleaning, as no grounds to be a public matter.

The people are tired I say, (They are tired of what) -- They are tired of being brought by politics.

We came together in 2008, and worked hard –voted and created a symbol of change. And nobody said that this type of change would be easy, nobody said that changing the makeup of this country was going to happen overnight. And nobody said that working from the bottom up was going to dramatically change federal, state, or municipal government in one session, or year. And nobody anticipated a congressional house, and senatorial republicans—to be insubordinate on the growth of this country, in order to tank it, and make sure our president fails. And the leadership of John Boehner shouldn't be about a copy-paste movement to swift vote the general public. And from day one, a lot of people who would never vote for, or have voted for President Barack Obama, wanted to make his presidential legacy—an ilegentiment president. Where they have gone as far as disrespecting the office of the president?

The people are tired I say, (They are tired of what) -- They are tired of being brought by politics.

Men, and women—young and old, baby boomers, next generation to generation x – this culture to demonize our leaders in a landscape of divide and conquer must come to an end in our spectrum of politics. It's a major pointing factor for our leaders to act with respect to those elected to office.

Since the people who vote in these elections, would like those running to lead our government; would like to see a unified front. The people are tired of the type of politics that divide and deter people away from engaging in politics.

The people are tired I say, (They are tired of what) -- They are tired of being brought by politics.

If one man can inspire a group of people to change, and those groups of people can inspire others to change—we all as the people in this public of the United States can change.

I am fired up! I am ready to Go! If one man can change a candidate, and one candidate change a state, as one state can change a country—just imagine what one country can do to change the world.

After that speech, and making sure that we keep the people more evolved in this critical time in our elections and campaigns. Since this election because of the Citizen's United – we are looking at more money, more influence and more engagement in politics. Like people wanted to know what the Supreme Court ruling that allows (Super PACs) to raise and spend enormous amounts of money on presidential campaigns. In the year of 2012—we have seen some of the worse negative advertisements, and candidates breaking the rules, going outside the box, to swift vote these current elections. You see a lot of pandering and begging for votes. As the Republican Party has been come an isolated party! So this election is a critical step, and ideological route—we as Americans would like to choose.

This next speech is about which way you want this country to go. And the freedoms and liberties that we seek, on which direction—the union would like to go. This Speech is called: "State of the Union – where America will go?"

State of the Union – Where America will Go?

It was over 200 years when one of our leaders, as the president – made a statement. Four Scores and seven years ago; we the people are the victors of this country. A country that had half-free, and half-slave; plus a country where women, where the property of their men! We have come so far in our fight for justice and history, to allow the mongering of fear, and economic collapse – to send our country back into the years beyond the Four Scores' speech. Our union has never been stronger—the economic divide although has a bleak sign in the recovery—has been a bright spot for our union. This Union, which is a free democratic society and have civil liberties that we so desperately take advantage of—are strong. A strong country has leaders who believe in their current leader. A strong union is a republic that respect the office of the president.

I'm a leader – you're a leader: let's lead to inspire and unite.

I implore you to fight for these civilian rights—rights that we have worked so hard to achieve. Before the speech "Four Scores," came about women couldn't vote—had no personal rights to their health, had to be submissive to their men. Before the speech: "Four Scores," came about – little children were allowed to work in mines. And the wages of our indentured servants, where a few cents on the dollar— while the tariffs where more expensive than its today! And half of the country was free, while the other half was slave. And majority of the population in these half free—half slave states, where inter-racial. And their rights were violated because of these notions that brought them to the middle.

I'm a leader -- you're a leader, let's inspire and unite.

Campaigns for leadership roles are about leaders uniting the electric—to believe and hope that we the people of this free union; can come together. Come together and move this country forward; in a way were the people are respected for the contributions that are put into this country. And come together, on making sure that our fruits and labors benefit the lives of the poor, economical disadvantage—prosperous individuals, plus super rich – on reaping the benefits of what this country has harvested and Sheppard. We need our growth on democracy to continue its growth, and be the model symbol—for other countries to invest interest on. People won't invest in America or Americans from another country—if our leaders are disrespecting the office of the President. Women's health and rights wouldn't have the pride that other females in other nations so desperately seek—if our leaders, weren't respecting their mothers, and daughters. We live in a free democratic country that we the people have fought hard to achieve.

I'm a leader – you're a leader; let's inspire and unite

I want to unite you the people, those who are republican, with those that are democrats—on coming together with those that are independent, in order to represent our democratic state. A state where we have so many free rights and freedoms, that we as the people in the public take advantage of without notice. Since together, the people united will never be defeated, and one unified country, with the public and the people that respect our president in: President Barack Obama, just imagine what obstacles we can overcome together. One Nation, were the people can believe in the fight, the vibe or the rights to dream big, and work hard—to Sheppard a product, where it will bring prosperity to all.

We don't need to go back to the days, where our women hung out in closets – to take the life out of their bodies, because they were afraid of religious persecution.

We don't need to go back to the days, where labor was free for half of the population and less than a few cents for those who migrated to this country.

We don't need to back to the times – where our leaders where disrespecting our president.

We don't need to divide the country in order to win an election.

We don't need a solution where we have three separate states of the union – haves and have knots, entitled and title less to elected and non elected.

We don't need to fall into a state, where corruption—placed with bad leaderships, becomes the doorways and gates to a poverish state.

We don't need to see a principal statement as: "We are broke," in order to invest in the same securities that made this the most prosperous nation in the world.

No! We want our people to unite, respect, believe and achieve.

Believe in the notion that an education, hard work and organization, can create a narrative of a story, where a poor man in the delta, can travel to New York City—while getting the same rights as everyone else. Rights that leads to economic prosperity and social security on individual affairs.

Respect the will of the people, and the offices of our leaders! Respect the voices that go unheard, and allowing those who have on having a chance at the American Dream. And most importantly, respect our President of the United States. He's earned that much!

Achieve, in order for our country to achieve those same goals written in our constitution—we must achieve peace. We need to be at peace with thy neighbor, and be at peace with thy race, sex and creed. When the people are united— we can never be defeated, and that's what we must achieve.

Unite, now is the time more than ever to unite for one cause: Our Leaderships' respect, and the people living in this country.

I'm a leader – you're a leader; let's inspire to unite.

Today, being a leader in a world full of leaders who makes appearances as leaders as in this century leadership are the new prophets – yet with no religious ties to any belief. I wrote that speech, to inspire the elected leaders, and those that inspire to lead, on leading the electric. Yet, the people were looking for leadership and they were begging for real leaders to come about and lead. And that inspired me to write that speech, since I proclaimed myself, and trademarked the title of The Next Generation of Leaders. And I made it a public display for the millions of followers whom like to read my jargons on social networks. So writing that speech and allowing it to go viral as all of the world leaders saw the imprints of the speech—not sure if they actually read it. But they have heard or read scripts of that speech made this movement on occupying the streets a tangible movement.

The movement to occupy the world will continue, and the story will be told by other voices, both men and women. Women more in particular have been the back bone of the OWS movement. They have been organizing, and hosting event while coming out to the rallies deep. I mean sometimes when I would appear to these rallies—there are more women in the rallies then they are men. Going to the rallies I thought it would be man on man in a battle with the police. But it turned out to be women in front of men, fighting off the police. But the police got tough, and started striking women, I was heated about the fact that men would use force on women. So I pushed to the front, and used my muscles to compel the women to hold the police at bay. And the more I push forward, the more people joined to create a human barricade. This made the movement grow, as more people started to come, and more men stood behind women, pushing the barricade forward. Yet, who would allow their women to sting in front of the lines. But there was no choice, the women ran the show, and all the men could do was be the wall from behind, so that the police didn't over power them.

I believed in the Malcolm X Shabazz, tact of using force with applied force. Malcolm got that strategy form Gandhi when they met resistance with resistance—yet, in my part; I had women. The Occupy Wall Street movement was and will always be about the women. This whole movement started with a person burning their self to disgrace their culture about how women were being treated, and how his country was treating him. The rallies, the fighting, the marching had a line of women that out weighted the men and even though more men were arrested than the women because of the force by the people on the NYC Police. The entire movement was based on the participation of women, and the organizational status of these women. Then the movement grew from men and women, to veterans helping women, to leaders pushing on getting to the front lines.

I even tried to find the sole leader who was a female in order to document and record her travels, with the fighting and mixture of how women inspired leaders to participate in this movement. Since it many of them were losing their economic wealth because of the fact that they are women. And banks like Chase Bank, Bank of America—used fraudulent practices on them and placing them in jeopardy of a financial personal meltdown. People didn't know or didn't fully understand the impacts that the mortgage crisis placed on women. Since majority of them were either female veterans, that used Chase Bank in purchasing their homes before they went off to fight for our country, and were coming back to huge mortgage bills, from equity loans. Some of the loans, they didn't fully understand; as people talk about the mortgage crisis, but nobody put a face on who was effected by the crisis—until this movement came about. The mortgage crisis was about men losing their homes that they went and fought for in fighting for their country—on their mothers' principals.

Chase ran a scheme on veterans whom purchased home equity loans, and couldn't keep up with the payments or the notes because of them handling their affairs overseas. And because of that most of the payments and funds from the federal government became delayed if these veterans didn't relist when they came home. And some of the veterans who needed the extra help, and financial advice or some type of income once they became veterans was non-existent in the economy of 2010. Because of the congressional war on budget cuts—congress managed to cut so much of the budget, and directed it too the defense system. They in directly placed people who were above water, under water and just because of the men and women who enlisted in our defense system, didn't fight overseas doesn't mean they weren't veterans.

And a lot of women, were those who where domestic veterans found themselves in trouble with the mortgages. And a lot of mothers of veterans fighting overseas also found themselves in trouble with their mortgages. And the problem became a clear cut crisis that even those who monitored the housing market, saw coming—yet, didn't see it coming in the direction that it came. They predicted that the housing bubble would halt, and fade the balloon—yet; they didn't expect the deflation to come from domestic and overseas veterans.

Which is why many of those that participated in the movement called: Occupy Wall Street – rallied and marched to the beat? They were pushed to the edge and nobody cared or was listening to them. They were forced to become a merchant of the oppressed. So they all had one thing in comment—which was no respect from the government, and the unhappiness with banks. And that unhappiness put boots to asses, as people drove the wave. And I will always say it – I, Omar Dyer wasn't and isn't the leader of the Occupy Wall Street movement. I'm not the face of the movement, and the only thing that I done was give them the blitz and media circus that they needed.

The movement had its promise and it has down falls, and the battle of who controlled the big city in New York City has now begun. And as you know Omar Dyer, whom has this Pen-Name, called TheFanNJ, like to end his memoirs with a leading into the next story for his journey in politics. It became the perception of Omar Dyer a.k.a. TheFanNJ verses the New York City Police: with Police Commissioner Ray Kelly, and Mayor Mike Bloomberg. People know how big and bad the New York City police department is, and the limits they will go in order to carry out their policing agenda.

Chapter 5

TheFanNJ: Omar Dyer v
New York City elected

As a black man coming from the state of New Jersey, and being an activist, who made political leaders crumble. Omar Dyer had the political clout to make a local leader pull his hair out. After the march on Wall Street, which shut down the NYC financial center of exchange for 15 minutes? Congressman Peter King, created a bogus file, and started a political rumor based on non-creditable information on the name of a person. Omar Lomant Dyer has the same name which cross references with names on the terrorist watch list. This is a list that can single out anyone for making comments in the public against the government, which was assigned by the Patriot Act. Well, in order to decrease and scare people from joining the protest with Omar Dyer, congressman Peter King filed a report about Omar Dyer being one to watch.

Omar Dyer is no stranger to controversy since: TheFanNJ wrote a book that was nominated for 3 awards, including a pre-nomination to a Nobel. Well, he was selected in pre-nomination for the Nobel, and failed to reach the final round of 5 rounds. That book attacked: the former President George W. Bush called: America's War. TheFanNJ went after the former president on his role with how he handled Hurricane Katrina. And it was a public battle that made literary commentary on the president— where he wrote his rebuttal book. Former President G.W. Bush knew that a writer wasn't really a danger to his health or administration. Yet, Congressman Peter King whose the chairman of the Homeland Security—which shares and set the information for prospective activities to go monitored, felt that making a political statement—while placing names on list, that have nothing to do with the idea of terror. Was a battle that Congressman Peter King, didn't think he would be in a battle to lose. The old vow to make African American Leaders, labeled terrorist – strike rumors to monitor and terrorize people's financial accounts were there in the 60's. In closed doors, Hoover harassed and mocked, made attempts to embarrass Dr. Reverend Martin Luther King Jr.

And every attempt the leaders in Washington, DC wanted to make Dr. Reverend Martin Luther King Jr. irrelevant, with bogus rumors that weren't true. And those rumors that weren't challenged and met, finally caught up to Reverend Martin Luther King Jr.

How does this match up to Omar Dyer, and his pen-name, TheFanNJ. Well, because of his high profile and the ability to use social media in drawing massive crowds to an event. Congressman Peter King wanted to kill the threat. So he placed the name of Omar Lomant Dyer on most-likely to watch list. And stated that the name is making threats against the government that can comprise the integrity of the security of the country, and yes, Congressman Peter King is now in panic mode. After Times Magazine made "The Protestor," their person of the year, everyone wanted to know the person behind the movement. Well, they've found their target when Occupy Wall Street had four marches that shut down traffic, and shut down the city for more than an hour. Yes, they gave that title to Omar Lomant Dyer: and I automatically was placed on this secret list. And then I was labeled as an Islamic practitioner because of the people that hung in my circle. Even though I am a one circle representative – they thought that would scare people from following my messages, or appearing to the events that I would cast. And that would stop organizations from doing work, or make it harder for them to invest in Omar Lomant Dyer.

So I incorporated myself, and created patens in the state of New Jersey to protect myself from invaders and crusaders. Yet, that wasn't stopping them from shutting up my mouth –since pay by performance sites drove my message. They then drafted a law, called NDAA (National Defense Authorization Act) which gave government the rights to monitor American Citizens, and then give the right to kill them if they consider that person a threat to the security of the country. This law was drafted to stop, companies from allowing information or messages to be spread over the internet. And it was clear on who was the target when they drafted this law. It was directed to assassinate any leader who can stir up the people, and had the same power as Dr. Reverend Martin Luther King Jr. and don't have the financial background, and was a nuisance to how the government treated it's people.

Believe me or call me crazy, but this law the NDAA that was drawn up, was directed to those who they considered leaders of the Occupy Wall Street movement. And many of those that follow the movement who wanted to protect those that they believe in always said that—Occupy Wall Street has no real leader. Yet, the government and their list makers don't care about who those that follow are trying to protect. They are more worried about the person that can bring them to the table, and interfere with how they govern. Congressman Peter King, was looking for a way to assassinate me, and using this clause to push through legislation and on giving the president a bogus file to kill an American Citizen. They can create a file distort the truth, place a sheer of doubt in the public eye – call whomever they see as a threat to their interest a terrorist, and send the President of the United States a file that is incomplete, and ask for that president to pull the trigger on killing an American Citizen.

And to back up the claims of using this agenda—they will use other incidents to draw in and ran on that they have vital information. But I am Omar Lomant Dyer, I fear no man, and no government – plus I don't fear any president even if he was my mentor, or friend. I personally don't like Eric Holder: the U.S. Attorney General – since he doesn't represent the community in which he came from. He's the face and imprint yet he doesn't represent the struggle of the African American Community. And instead of coming to help—he defected to the theories made up by Congressman Peter King. I have been given a gift to lead people, and many of the times—when you have a great gift, you tend to get enemies.

Well, this became a serious issue, when I had my challenges with police commissioner Ray Kelly. Since Ray Kelly never seen a person like Omar Lomant Dyer. He's never seen a person with the will, and passion to defy the odds. Police Commissioner Ray Kelly went on radio and said that the occupy movement can't and will not disrupt the flow of traffic if came to New York City's biggest state: Time Square. And we challenged them, and shut down the traffic concerns and liabilities during our three marches on Time Square. And I went on radio, or robo-call that I will challenge him to arrest me during an occupy protest. And he couldn't, which ticked him off even more because many of his own members of his department stated to question his authority. They started to believe in my leadership, and ability to lead then his own, rights to deprive the people of their freedom of speech.

So when he sent information to Congressman Peter King on a person of interest. They wanted to stop people from coming into New York City, and holding up traffic – they wanted to stop the Union and trade organizations from supporting Omar Lomant Dyer, and the Occupy Wall Street movement by any means necessary. Even if that includes, making a bogus report, to kill a person of interest.

New York City police Commissioner Ray Kelly, had his crew follow me around. He had private investigators tap into my finances—harass the place I would eat at, monitor and list the events I would attend. And invade my privacy because they wanted to monitor my every move. Yet, that didn't stop there – my phone lines were tapped. And how do I know my line was monitored, you would get a beeping sound every time I made a phone call. And it seemed like the entire would knew every conversation I had before I hung up the phone. Then my Apple note-pad was hacked into, and all of my files were copied and recorded. My website was hacked and crashed countless times, and my information became free for the public to see.

My business went into an audit review, where every file became an incomplete file—and I had to pay fines and fees. This made it very difficult to do business, since other businesses wouldn't want to do business – because they would be audited by the Internal Revenue Services, and charged fees and fines that were simply made up. Where they created the delays, they created the problems and they inflected a financial hardship in order to take away assets and values from Omar Lomant Dyer?

Well, I went on the attack, wrote blogs—posted on Facebook about how I know; plus believe and see that Congressman Peter King (being a racist) and Police Commissioner Ray Kelly wanted to assassinate me. And it's very true because from the moment I felt that vibe that government or leaders representing government wanted to kill me. I would cry, every time I would standout and march with the protestors. Even though I knew that I was the target, it didn't stop me from marching for people's civil liberties. You can call me crazy, or you don't have to believe in the words that I am writing.

But you can't shadow out that perception and doubt, that when someone non-elected that challenges local government and is able to draw massive amounts of people to believe in their perception – leaders in government would, work on details to end that movement or terminate the target. And it's very much true that Omar Lomant Dyer was the defined target of the New York City Police Department (they wanted to kill me). Why, I did something no other leader could ever do: forced the New York City Police Department to buckle, made members in the department join me in a march—took the controls of the police department away from their leaders. And that's why I was a threat, not because of I was with the Occupy movement—it was more because I was taking the charge from the police commissioner and he wanted that back. He wanted the perception of control back. And he declared war on protestors from Occupy Wall Street.

How did this fight with TheFanNJ reach Mayor Mike Bloomberg? Well, he's the mayor of New York City – and there's people crying about how the protestors are interrupting the flow of the city. So he's the leader, and this was an attack on his administration. Plus he's looking at his poll numbers going down. Here's a history lesson for you: Mayor Mike Bloomberg, before the battle with his police commissioner became a problem: donated and supported: Omar Lomant Dyer: a.k.a. TheFanNJ. But it became a problem of do I support my personal choice on who I appointed to this position, or do I support a leader that I like. Mayor Bloomberg made the choice to support his staff. And that made the artist: TheFanNJ create a song called – "Take Back Congress," which went viral. And that song, which was satire on the city of New York, where it said: "Bloomberg beware, there's occupants everywhere."

As it hit the billboard charts, Congress lead by Congressman Peter King, did what everything he could to try and stop this song from being distributed. And by creating the Stop Online Piracy Act—gave them the right to prevent companies from displaying the work. Which stopped online websites like YouTube, and any other pay per performance for displaying this song? That didn't stop me from using social media to attack the Mayor on his policy. The major problem is or was that they made a choice to take out the target, and answer to questions later.

What happened, whom ever was assigned to take the shot couldn't take the shot. And how did I know that they had a target on me. It's simple, as the march got to the Sheraton Hotel, and all of the leaders came to support the President. When the President saw the number of people, protesting the event? The President left, and couldn't participate in the event. Then around 9:10pm on that same day – you can see the video on my Facebook. People started screaming, and yelling about a police officer on the room. They started moving away from me, and then a red light struck me dead in the eye.

I wasn't scared but what I did was staring directly at the officer on the roof, and looked into his heart. And dared the officer to take the shot (without saying one word), call me crazy, and say that I am making stuff up; yet I know that they wanted to take out the target. And I gave them a target to take out—if they wanted to make me the honorary leader of the movement, and wanted to make an example; I personally didn't care anymore. Then I wanted to look directly into the eye of the person holding the responsibility to shot the target.

Because if this wasn't a real threat, or an order to take out the target why was that person stationed on that part of the roof in the first place. Why did the New York City Police go to extreme measures to ward off people, from knowing what was going on? Why did the police department need 13 huge sanitation trucks, to close off the people? Why did they close people in after I entered the area? Why wouldn't they answer any question or ignored me or anyone that was around me during that 2 hour time span? Why did they stop traffic from going into that area for three hours? Why was the reporting news required to move from the area? Why did they allow some people to leave, and others weren't allowed to leave during that time?

Those are serious questions, since that's the makings of an attempt to kill someone or take out a target. Nobody would go to those measures on bringing 13 huge dump trucks to block the view of the people. Then close of the block, so nobody can get into that area. While placing an officer on the balcony of the restaurant that was in the Hotel! And then have 200 or more police officers surrounding the area, with no instructions and not willing to answer anyone. Use barricades to block people and hold them against their will, for what purpose. And not take out the target or the officer assigned to take out the target, get his soul read where he can't take out the target. And if I am making stuff up, then maybe someone should start to tell me some answers.

And not cover up the elements of facts, that I was a target – as they in government wanted to take me as a person out.

Since this was the only event that went to those measures. It was the only chance that the Mayor Mike Bloomberg, police commissioner Ray Kelly, and Congressman Peter King had, and it failed. They knew that they couldn't take out the target, and answer questions on who the target was, once the target known that the target became the target. And this wasn't the last event that was held by Occupy Wall Street—where they protested the President of the United States in New York City. There were many others, and many more where the police didn't close off the area – block the people from getting to the protestors, stop traffic—place an officer on the roof top; with a weapons hot signal. Plus, use 13 huge sanitation truck, to block the view of the public—while the use of barricades to detain people from entering or leaving the area for 3 hours.

Occupy Wall Street organized three more protest that were directed to protest against the President of the United States in 2011. And I was scheduled to show up and protest—where I didn't show up. And because I didn't show up at those protest, there was no police presences, no barricades, no extra security—or anyone mounting roof tops with assault riffles' with a weapons hot tag. There was no target, and the media was allowed to interview all 100 people that shown up. As I raise these questions, and ask my readers one simple thing – if this wasn't an attempt by the New York City police department, and police commissioner Ray Kelly sole mission to assassinate me; (Omar Lomant Dyer) then what was the display of force and military style for – as if I am not trained on the order of operation on how to detect force.

I plotted out their attempt to close people off as I ranted and raved about how this is an illegal detain. I then started to warn people about how the police were moving in—as some people started to leave the area. They then allowed the merchant to leave, as other escaped with him.

And once I noticed that the officer on the roof was setting up, and had his gun directly pointed at me. I then noticed that people started to stand far away from me as possible, as they started to sit on the ground—or in corners or areas making me a wide open target instead of a shadow in the crowd. I don't care about what anyone would say or the implications of the matter—even whatever the leaders who drew up the orders have to say about what I am talking about. I was the target when it comes to this movement from Occupy Wall Street, and regardless of who the movement thinks are the leaders, they wanted to assassinate me.

And to be truthful, members of Occupy Wall Street really didn't agree with me, or wanted to be associated with me. I was just someone that can bring a lot of people to their events. And that's what I was being used for. People donated to the movement because of the perception that I was a part of the management. When I had no direct connection, to any of the organizations involved in the Wall Street Occupy Movement? Can you imagine that this whole notion of Occupy Wall Street, was a standing stage of Omar Dyer's political career beginning in New York City.

And if you think about any political leader, or political activist – maybe even a political operative; this was Omar Dyer's first challenge and coming out stage in New York City. The biggest city in America, Omar Dyer set the record books. The pen-name joined Occupy Wall Street, and shut down New York City, and changed the political climate in New York City, brought issues that NYC leaders couldn't bring to the fore-front. With the movement from Occupy Wall Street, and the members of the vow to fight against government, abusing the rights of the people— Omar Dyer was able to challenge the status quo.

You have to understand, Omar Dyer was relativity known around the globe, as a former gubernatorial candidate for the great state of New Jersey. And a long time friend of the Mayor in Mike Bloomberg became a public run-a-way that was a threat to the administration.

And making the issue about the brutality of the New York City police department a national discussion, and at first the media really didn't want to give Omar Dyer any credit. They didn't want to make it seem as if the internet blogger had anything to do with the massive movement sweeping: New York City. They didn't expect that other unions, and political leaders would join the party on economic equality. And let's be honest, nobody really understood the leadership qualities that Omar Dyer held. And I say this as the writer of this memoir and in third person because of the fact – nobody was giving any credit to the level of Impact Omar Dyer had on the political landscape: Occupy Wall Street, with the advocacy of Omar Dyer, has done in New York City.

For a small limit of time Omar Dyer with the Occupy Wall Street movement actually took over New York City. No political pundit, no candidate – no advocate has ever taken over the Manhattan Borough as Omar Dyer, with the help of Occupy Wall Street has done. No person or group lead with or by an advocate has ever taken over Time Square in New York City. No person, and no group, has ever taken over: The American Stock Exchange on Wall Street in New York City. And no leader has ever been able to use a group, and organize a worldwide protest on civil liberties as Omar Dyer has done, with the help of Occupy Wall Street. And let us be very clear, this was Omar Dyer's first appearance in New York City.

It was his first stride to march against corporate policies that lead to the terminology of the 99%. Remember, people have heard of Omar Dyer as President Barack Obama's supporter. They knew of him, and many of them wanted to stay away from him – but as the marching and protesting in New York City grew, it was really clear that Omar Dyer has become the biggest opponent to Mayor Mike Bloomberg. It was song skeptical that Omar Dyer used TheFanNJ to create a song about Mayor Mike Bloomberg. A song that topped the billboard charts, and made iTunes song of the week which was called: "Take Back Congress."

As I close this memoir and rehash the memories of my ride with Occupy Wall Street, in my first political appearance in New York City. I can say I left a mark in the history books that no other leader, political candidate, advocate – plus group of leaders could have done, or have done—in order to change the spectrum on policy making and public perception in New York City. This was the first stage of Omar Dyer as a political pundit to make hay-day of public elected leaders.

And as I make my mark in New Jersey, and set the stage for the newest collection in my memoirs and journey to become the Next Generations Leader in my movement as: The Next Generation of Leaders Movement. We've done something that nobody has ever done, in politics and policy in New York City, and New York in general – which was take over the biggest and major parts of the biggest city in the world. Can you imagine someone coming into your town, taking over you most famous block or section – and out-stage your own mayor and police commissioner; to a point where they want you to move to that city, and be their mayor, speaks volumes about what has happened? And I think history, will tell the story, that a young 32 year old first time around, young candidate – is that leader, this Generation has been looking for. And I hate to be the only person writing this story about the leadership qualities of what Omar Dyer using the pen-name: TheFanNJ, and joining up with Occupy Wall Street.

The End or the beginning

WE ARE ONE

About the Author:
TheFanNJ: Omar Dyer

Omar Dyer became one of the best writers in America after he created the pan name called TheFanNJ. After that the pen-name TheFanNJ was the most nominated author since Mark Twain. And on the internet using social media like Facebook, Myspace, and Google. Omar Dyer and his pen-name became an online reality show in politics, sports, and community outreach. Omar Dyer has a Doctor's of philosophy degree. He went to Kaplan University and achieved a Masters in Legal Studies, a B.A. in Technical Writing in Communication – an A.A. in Child Development, and from the Children's Institution of Literature he has a degree in Teenage / children movie making in literature.

TheFanNJ was a pen-name created by Omar Dyer in 2004 – which has grown in a social media environment. Omar Dyer is a novelist that has written speeches and advocate for social justice and humanity around the world. Omar Dyer is a former campaign organizer for President Barack Obama. He's used the pen-name TheFanNJ to mark one of the biggest protests in American History known as the Occupy Wall Street movement. Although the title of the book is Wall Street Occupied, because of copyrights and play rights – TheFanNJ wrote his side of the story on this movement called: Wall Street Occupied. This is his story on the events that happened during the 2011 protests, from the infamous march on the policies of New York Mayor's Mike Bloomberg, with the famous fight back with the New York City Police at Time Square – all the way to the liberation in Libya, and the fight to free the people of Syria. This movement has defined Omar Dyer as the people's champ, and political activist of this generation. Which gave the entire movement that title from Time's magazine "Person of the Year;" THE PROTESTOR? And since they couldn't find one person to mark, or find TheFanNJ – even though he drew the crowds, they gave the entire movement that title. And this is the story of Wall Street Occupied.

Notes:

Notes:

Notes: